Masterpieces of Costume Jewelry

Joanne Dubbs Ball
&
Dorothy Hehl Torem

77 Lower Valley Road, Atglen, PA 19310

Library of Congress Cataloging-in-Publication Data

Ball, Joanne Dubbs.
Masterpieces of costume jewelry / J. Ball & D. Torem.
p. cm.
Includes bibliographical references and index.
ISBN 0-88740-900-8 (hard)
1. Costume jewelry. I. Torem, Dorothy Hehl. II. Title.
NK4890.C67B366 1995
739.27–dc20   95-31294
CIP

Copyright © 1996 by
Joanne Dubbs Ball & Dorothy Hehl Torem

Photographs by Dorothy Hehl Torem

All rights reserved. No part of this work may be reproduced or used in any forms or by any means graphic, electronic or mechanical, including photocopying or information storage and retrieval systems without written permission from the copyright holder.

Printed in Hong Kong
ISBN: 0-88740-900-8

We are interested in hearing from authors
with book ideas on related topics.

Published by Schiffer Publishing Ltd.
77 Lower Valley Road
Atglen, PA 19310
Please write for a free catalog.
This book may be purchased from the publisher.
Please include $2.95 postage.
Try your bookstore first.

Dedication

This book is dedicated to Milton Torem, a gentleman whose devotion was all encompassing. He was devoted to his adored wife Dorothy Hehl Torem and to his children and grandchildren, to the country he served during World War II–and in that service became a war hero–and to the jewelry industry, where he is regarded as a legend, and to which he devoted over forty years of his distinguished life.

Acknowledgments

With appreciation to the following for their assistance: Bob Ball; Davida Baron and Lucille Tempesto, "Vintage Fashion and Costume Jewelry Newsletter"; Michelle Breslin, DMM Federated Dept. Stores; Kerry Cerio and Sharon White, Tempo Designs, East Greenwich, R.I.; Michele Courtois; Charles Edwards; Elizabeth Gary; Ginger Moro; Juliet Weber Reid; Bob Simas and Paul Rerick, East Greenwich Photo Lab, East Greenwich, R.I.; Alyson Torem-French; Jake Torem; Milton Torem; and Stanley Zukowski.

With special thanks to those who shared their collections with us: Jeanine Davis, Portsmouth, Virginia; Ben Cassara, Fourty Fifty Sixty, New York; Jeannie Graf Roberts, Robert's Antiques, Micanopy, Florida; Linda Rosen Vangel; Catherine Stein, Catherine Stein, Inc., New York; Linda Thibedeau, Razzle Dazzle, Cambridge, Massachusetts; and Eve Savitt, New York City.

Our deep appreciation also to family members and associates of these "costume jewelry giants" who shared knowledge, and in some cases, family jewelry and mementos with us: Nancy Agnini Brady; Joyce Chorbajian; Karl Eisenberg; Frank Fialkoff of Miriam Haskell, New York; Bob and Jim Hobe; Joan Castle Joseff; Jill Rader-Levine; Jon Levine; Bernard Shapiro; and Vivienne Westwood.

Contents

1 In the Eye of the Beholder 9
2 Faux Treasures: An Historical Perspective 11
    From Ancient to Classical 11
    The Nineteenth Century and Victoriana 16
    Brass and Glass 22
    Art Nouveau to Art Deco and Beyond 25
    The Couture Connection 31
3 The Techniques and Processes 33
    Enameling 34
    –Champlevé 35
    –Basse Taille 35
    –Cloisonné 36
    –Plique-à-jour 36
    –Repousse 37
4 A Gem of a Gem 39
5 The Factory and Workshop 41
    The Tools 41
    The Metals and Plating Process 41
    Molds, Castings, Findings and Fittings 42
6 The Artist and Craftsman 45
    Rendering 45
    Model Making 46
7 Marked and Memorable 49
    Designers and Manufacturers From A-Z ....
    Accessocraft 50
    American Style 50
    Art 50
    McClelland Barclay 51
    Bijoux Cascio 53
    Boucher 54
    Brania 56
    Burks 56
    Cadoro 56
    Calvaire 57
    Hattie Carnegie 57
    Castlecliff 60
    Alice Caviness 63
    Chanel 63
    Ciner 70
    Coro 71
    Vendome 76
    Francoise 77
    DeLillo 78
    De Mario 79
    De Rosa 79
    Di Nicola 80
    Mimi di N 81
    Eisenberg 82
    Eugene 91
    Florenza 91
    Givenchy 92
    Leo Glass 93
    Har 93

    Haskell 94
    Hobé 100
    Hollycraft 107
    Isadora 108
    Joseff of Hollywood 109
    Korda 118
    Kramer 119
    Kenneth Jay Lane 120
    Leiber 125
    Les Bernard, Vogue, and Ledo 125
    Lisner 129
    Mazer 130
    Monet 131
    Napier 131
    ORA 132
    Panetta 135
    Pennino 135
    Lucien Picard 136
    Pauline Rader 136
    Regency 138
    Reinad 138
    Reja 139
    Robert 139
    Nettie Rosenstein 144
    Yves Saint Laurent 148
    Sandor 149
    Schiaparelli 151
    Schreiner 160
    Selro 166
    Adele Simpson 167
    Trifari 168
    Vogue Bijoux 174
    Volupte 175
    Weisner 176
    Weiss 177
    Whiting and Davis 178
8 Unsigned Beauties of the Modern Era 179
9 Newer...and Notable 195
    Karl Lagerfeld 195
    Thelma Deutsch 196
    Vivienne Westwood 197
    Alexis LeHellec 198
    Lazaro 198
    Mark Spirito 199
    Isabell Canovas 200
    Adjani Moini 201
    Elsa Peretti 202
    Butler and Wilson 202
    Erickson Beamon 202
Bibliography 204
Price Guide 205
Index 207

"In the Eye of the Beholder"

Masterpiece: *A work done with extraordinary skill; a supreme intellectual or artistic achievement.*
-Webster's New Collegiate Dictionary

Like beauty, a "masterpiece" can also be in the eye of the beholder, and takes many forms. If one is a literary buff, Shakespeare most surely comes to mind. Then again, the words of Chaucer, Milton, Fitzgerald, Hemingway, or Steinbeck might rank high on one's home library of "must haves." For music buffs, the supreme masterpiece could cover the gamut from Mozart and Puccini to "Stardust" or The Beatles; and for those who covet a great painting, the mere thought of owning an original Renoir, Dufy, Van Gogh, Sargent, or even Warhol, can bring a tear to the eye...and a smile to the heart!

All this by way of emphasizing that when it comes to any art form, including jewelry, tastes vary and what one individual considers the ultimate "work of art," another may initially find simply uninteresting or overblown. In the jewelry category, bias against "costume jewelry"–that is, jewelry made with glass or imitation stones and non-precious settings–causes some to refer to it as "junk jewelry." Nevertheless, it would be wise for those who appreciate beauty to consider the fine workmanship and innovative methods of design in "imitation" pieces just as they would in precious ones. Regardless of whether a piece particularly enchants the viewer at first glance, it would behoove them to take a long, second look.

Carrying this one step further, some individuals dislike replications of bugs, snakes, or animals accessorizing their clothing. Similarly, large flashy brooches might be off-putting to the less adventuresome, but close inspection could likely reveal intricacies of jewelry design at its finest, such as layers of glittering stones and crystals in a myriad of shapes and sizes, often arranged in mind-boggling patterns. Closer examination might also reveal playful and imaginative figurals, replete with fine enameling or ingenious use of stones. Even to the untrained eye, the patience required during the many stages necessary to fashion such a piece cannot be readily dismissed, and to the trained eye of the jeweler or designer, each step necessary to the process of creating this masterpiece is mentally constructed, step by step, with unabashed admiration.

Just as the works of countless great masters could be had for a pittance many years before their value as art had at last been acknowledged (for many an artist, unfortunately, a turn of events that often occurred years beyond their death), so too were countless masterpieces of marvelous costume jewelry originally available for mere pennies by today's standards.

As with many other objects from days past, the discovery of an appealing example of costume jewelry from long ago–and even not so long ago–creates a special excitement for the aficionado. How fortunate that many of these pieces can still be admired and appreciated. How fortunate, too, that individual preferences in jewelry are as varied as those in literature, music, art, and a plethora of other delights.

Defining the Terms

It is important to understand that the term "costume" jewelry has become a somewhat generic one. As used in this book, costume jewelry is that which is made with imitation and/or non-precious gems in non-precious settings. "Costume jewelry is in fact an entirely twentieth-century phenomenon; the term was first used in 1933 in the New Yorker magazine. Prior to that, it had been referred to in Vogue as 'dress ornaments' or 'craftsmen's jewelry.'"[1] Economic conditions and scientific advances were also combined to further advance the evolution of costume jewelry's history. At the turn of the century "imitation" was the key word for "other than fine" jewelry. Its purpose was solely to fool the eye. "Factors such as the removal of gold from general circulation in 1933, and the development of new metals and plastics in the late 19th-early 20th century signaled the rise in costume jewelry, and pieces which had elements of both real and costume."[2] However, there were designers a step ahead of their time, for a Vogue 1914 article reported on a Miss Strange who worked in ornamental jewelry and buttons and was "...particularly proficient at plique à jour enameling...the writer observed that the monetary value of such stones and settings was secondary to the "decorative merit of their colour.'"[3] Although Miss Strange worked in gold and silver with some precious and semi-precious stones, these offerings were still referred to as "decorative" and on the fringes of the couture market; it would be several years before they, along with brass and copper jewelry, would finally establish their niche.

The term "costume" was first associated with theatrical pieces worn by actresses in stage presentations. This definition broadened as jewelry design and manufacture for the mass market came into being in the 20th century. Some of the jewelry that also falls into this category is referred to as "fashion" jewelry, including pieces bearing the name of, or produced by, high fashion designers.

Some costume pieces include semi-precious, natural stones (i.e., amethyst, topaz, jade, etc.), as well as natural stones of lesser value, such as those from the quartz family. These pieces fall outside the generally accepted criteria for "fine" jewelry because they are not constructed of precious metals (gold or platinum) or precious stones, such as diamonds, rubies, or emeralds. In some cases, however, small precious stones (such as rubies) may be used for a minor accent, like the eye of an animal for example. Thus, the generally accepted definition for costume jewelry will be used here, even though it may apply to time frames when the term was not in general usage.

1 *Costume Jewelry in Vogue*, p. 13
2 *Inside Antiques*, October 1994, p. 18
3 *Costume Jewelry in Vogue*, p. 31

Faux Treasures:
An Historical
Perspective

From Ancient to Classical

The jewelers' art, along with its ensuing "masterpieces," is not limited by time for it was practiced, with much expertise, in ancient times. In one form or another, its magnetic attraction goes back at least 7,000 to 8,000 years and evidence continues to be uncovered suggesting that the time during which civilizations were capable of creating these baubles may encompass far more years than most historians and archaeologists had previously thought.

History is replete with mind-boggling tales and breathtaking pictorial examples of the enormous amounts of gold and precious gems with which bygone populations were laden. It, therefore, became inevitable that attendant economic and political conditions would play a role in the emergence of more modest adornments to satisfy the needs of those who were socially and financially less fortunate.

An understanding of past centuries and their class-conscious reliance on gold and fine jewels provides a valuable background for understanding the evolution of jewelry, with the modern and the past each interconnecting with the other. As geographic boundaries became less inhibitive and the world literally seemed to shrink in size, the stage was set for the eventual emergence of what was later referred to as simply "costume jewelry," an enormous accessorizing category that reached its apex in our own twentieth century.

The Industrial Revolution was perhaps primarily–albeit somewhat indirectly–responsible for costume jewelry's enthusiastic acceptance in the modern world, and its domino effect, which slowly but surely aided in the dissolution of many of the rigid class structures established earlier. A peek at what preceded this nineteenth century "revolution" will serve to set the stage for what was to later occur in the jeweler's art, when the world "turned the corner" into the twentieth century.

Through centuries past, precious and non-precious jewelry ran the gamut from simple ornamentation to pieces designed to distinguish rank in the social order...or even for their purported magical powers. Chief among the latter were amulets and talismans thought to endow the wearer with such diverse blessings as good health, great wealth, and long, even everlasting, life. An example of such a talisman are the "bishop rings," which date back to at least the early days of the 7th century and were believed to be endowed with such mystical qualities. Large and usually worn over the glove, they were also a symbol of authority, presented to an individual by the reigning monarch and supposedly returned to him on the wearer's death. What happened to the ring if the monarch "departed" first was apparently an unthinkable possibility, at least for the king!

Even more primitive jewelry has a distinctive charm that entitles it to a place in the "masterpieces" category. Simple decorative beads which frequently served as legal tender and were referred to as "trade beads" have an "in your face" beauty that makes a powerful statement for the utilization of vivid colors in simple but effective designs. Mosaic jewelry, and mosaic work in general, are prime examples of how the use of ordinary materials readily at hand can produce something beautiful and artistically noteworthy. Pieces of rough, irregularly-sized colored stones, and even marble were placed in all manner of patterns and designs resulting in objects ranging from handsomely primitive to amazingly intricate. Initially, the application was relatively simple, with some of the stones inlaid while others were merely cemented, often crudely, onto the surface.

When all is said and done, however, at the core of humankind's captivation with jewelry is a credo that comes as no surprise. Simply stated, "...attitudes to jewels developed from a simple love of anything shiny and colourful."[1] Each civilization and every empire left personal legacies behind, its unique fingerprints in time. From Egypt and Persia to Greece and Rome, from Etruscans and Minoans to Indians and Byzantines, the glory of jewelry was found everywhere, reconfirming and solidifying the human need to adorn, protect, and deify. Along with the ordinary details of daily life, jewelry also provides an opportunity to peer into the inner workings of the times and cultures in which it was created, for what people chose to wear or simply covet is a mirror that reflects those aged images back to us. Just as a parade of revolutionary inventions and innovative ideas have brought about graduated phases in the evolution of individual civilizations and mankind as a whole, so too do such seemingly everyday accoutrements as fashion and jewelry reflect the times that produced them.

Like fashion in general, elements of jewelry design go 'round and 'round in man's evolution. As the saying goes, imitation is the sincerest form of flattery. Indeed, "...any attractive object is rarely in the marketplace for long before it's copied or imitated."[2] This applies to the use of synthetic instead of genuine stones and to the designs themselves. The inspiration for many fashion and jewelry designs can be found in one form or another by a look back at far-flung ancient civilizations, and throughout various historical time periods, such as the Middle Ages and the Renaissance, right through the Victorian era and beyond. From one idea grows another, perhaps embellished, perhaps softened...a change here and there, updated for current lifestyles, and *voilà*, a "new" idea is reborn!

This decorative "reincarnation" is aptly demonstrated by the cupids and angels now enjoying a resurgence of interest, much as they did in Victorian times (even such luminaries as Mark Twain and his wife Olivia had four intricately carved cherubs "standing guard" on each post of the bedstead that they purchased in Venice in 1878). A look even farther back, however, will show that these charming figures had captured the peoples' fancy many centuries before, not only in classical paintings but also abundantly in what is often referred to as "classical jewelry."

The scarab, so indicative of Egyptian culture, has also time and again enjoyed renewed popularity. Today it is once again in demand just as it was during Edwardian times and the Deco period of the 1920s. In Egypt, the scarab originated as a stamp seal, "...mounted as a spindle on a ring, fixed on a pendant...or simply suspended round the neck on a silken thread...this was the classical universal charm or amulet, popular for burial as well as in life, so popular indeed that it was imitated by both the Greeks and the Etruscans."[3]

This obsession with death and the afterlife led to the strange but somehow comforting practice of creating glorious golden and bejeweled ornaments solely for the future enjoyment of the beloved departed as they embarked on their journey into the afterlife. It has been noted that many pieces of Ancient Greek and Etruscan jewelry are very delicate and thin, seemingly unsuitable for wear, providing further evidence that many "masterpieces" were fashioned to ornament a lifeless body and not to adorn the living.

Social and political idiosyncracies involving seemingly minor items played a role in many revealing scenarios. It was understandable that during the Middle Ages jewels only remained in the hands of the very wealthy. Nevertheless, rulers fearful of "underlings" upstaging them or appearing to compete felt compelled to issue edicts preventing the common folk from attempting to take on even the simplest of airs that might smack of royal "copycating." Here was insecurity at its most illogical–kings and queens actually felt threatened by those they ruled, not via political or military coups,

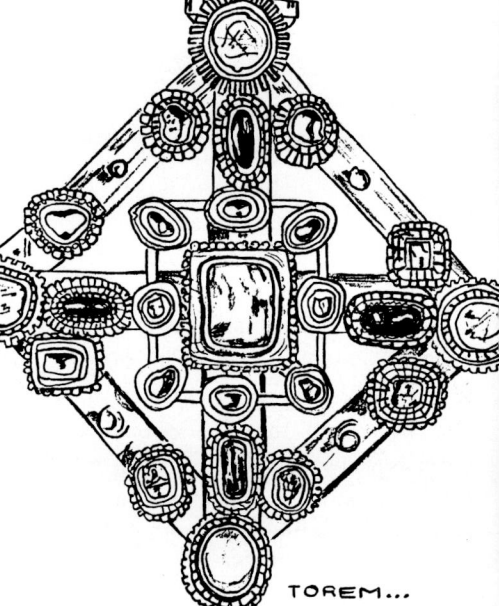

Byzantine cross from the 6th century, a design that proved to be inspirational to Chanel some fourteen centuries later.

but with pinky rings! During the 14th century, Edward III forbade subjects beneath a certain rank to wear rings, buckles, or any ornaments of precious stones. It is doubtful that he had much success in enforcing this edict, and restrictions aside, it was inevitable that when the balance of wealth at long last began to shift from royalty to commoners, the expansion of those accoutrements formerly only admired from afar made their way into society as a whole.

Known as the Classical Period, the seventeenth century "turned its back" on the magical influences of earlier jewelry. Now the elements of the stones overshadowed the designs, and the skillful cutting of gems was practiced, producing dazzling results. As a result the jewels overtook the settings rather than solely enhancing them as they had done in the past (as would be seen later in Art Nouveau, nature also played a major role in these designs). Here again, fashion and accessories went hand in hand, one influencing the other. The heavy, ponderous fabrics that once dominated had now been replaced by filmier materials like silks and laces. So as not to overpower this somewhat fragile look, delicate jewelry became a necessary adjunct to the female wardrobe.

The distinction between artist and craftsman was brought to the fore in the seventeenth century, and the field expanded to include many specialists. "Jewelers no longer sought to follow painting and sculpture, and abandoned historical and religious motifs, complex compositions and symbolism...the factors which restrained it in one direction set it free in another. What it lost in realism it gained in imagination, and this is possibly where its originality lies."[4] This was also the century that saw jewelry-making a slow but steady turn toward becoming more predominantly feminine, catering less to the males who had previously embraced it. Diamonds also rose to the forefront in the precious gems category, a status that has not been relinquished to this day. With more focus on faceted gems, the formerly popular cabochon styles were almost totally eliminated, and enameling also fell from favor.

In seventeenth century France, jewelry even played a role in high finance and economics and was considered a culprit in rises in the cost of living. This led to Sumptuary Laws that placed restrictions on the work of jewelers and in Germany a movement to reject the use of excessive jewelry gained momentum as well. Early in the century, Spain also enacted a sumptuary law prohibiting jewelry or ornamentation featuring any figures in relief, except for those of an ecclesiastical nature. Times were so restrictive, in fact, that even the number of stones in a given piece was limited. As

From 1765, a French paste hatpin.

in previous centuries, this too would pass, for history time and again has shown that when it came to accessorizing, the human species would not be denied, and as the century progressed, France once again became the center of influence for jewelry styles and designs. For instance, ribbon and bow designs–both individually and as part of more elaborate pieces--that became so popular in both fine and costume jewelry of later centuries, originated in France during this period.

The work of one man, sometimes referred to as a forerunner of Fabergé, came to prominence in the late seventeenth century--German born John Melchior Dinglinger. "His work ushers in one of the most brilliant periods in European jewelry...he was a goldsmith, a jeweler and an enameler, which was unusual in this period."[5] The works of Dinglinger also deviated from most jewelry of the period, many instead featuring designs having Chinese and Turkish overtones.

Reflecting the prominence placed on the stones as opposed to the settings, enormous numbers of pieces from the seventeenth century were unfortunately dismantled, and the gems simply transferred to other settings. Instead of actually viewing the pieces, as we have come to expect from other periods, much of our knowledge of the styles of this particular time is dependent upon studying the jewelry worn by those who sat for the portraits that were so commonly done then.

In eighteenth century Europe, class distinction, with its inherent fears of robbery, seems to have played a role in the increase in imitation pieces. An object of much thievery was the lowly shoe buckle. Since, for the most part, gentlemen had toned down their indulgence in the many jeweled adornments their forefathers had worn so lavishly, their shoe buckles took on a special significance...a "last stand," so to speak!

Of necessity, "...when they wanted to travel, they had to replace the ornaments on their shoes with something less valuable but no less showy. This may not be the origin of the large output of imitation jewels, which is also characteristic of eighteenth century England, but it is certainly a contributing factor."[6]

In the interest of nationalism during times of tumult and war, it became a patriotic but certainly painful gesture in the eighteenth century to sacrifice treasured family heirlooms to the national "cause." Consequently, jewelry comprised solely of crystals, and often made of steel, was worn to signify austerity, one's honor, and allegiance to country. In the process, the beauty to be found in more simple and less costly materials made tentative inroads in the long journey toward public acceptance of "costume" jewelry.

An early presentation of the "stars, moons, and planets" theme, indicative of the worldwide, centuries-old popularity of this recurring theme in jewelry design.

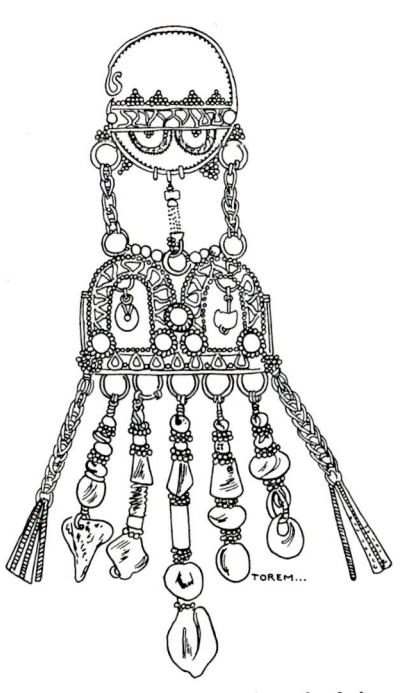

An ancient Byzantine design from the 3rd century.

The Nineteenth Century and Victoriana

As the eighteenth century gave way to the nineteenth, jewelry was punctuated by the sentimental. Portraits were centered in medallions, and cameos, mourning jewelry, even hair jewelry became popular with both the elite and the masses. There was also a revival in Renaissance and Gothic designs that reflected the mystique of exotic, foreign lands such as India and Africa. It was a century that could quite rightly be described as a veritable "melting pot" of jewelry.

The French Revolution effectively destroyed or considerably hindered the trade guilds, including the goldsmiths. With most craftsmen abandoning the family lineage that had been passed down to them, a rift was created between the artist's concept and the craftsman's interpretation. Those circumstances and the vagaries of fashion caused jewelry to lose some of the importance it had previously held. Additionally, many fortunes had been lost and jewels had to be sold, resulting in an ornament's value

tured in ornate and complex silver settings. Also found were crosses and large pendants suspended from long chains around the neck, much in the Medieval manner (a popular style in costume pieces of the 1990s). French "paste" was a somewhat tainted commodity, and looked down upon as an adornment chosen solely by actresses.

To enhance the hair of a Victorian lady, this aigrette bird is of French jet.

no longer being the sole criteria for its desirability. Glitter, and the attention it generated, was good enough for many and this, too, sounded the clarion call of "things to come."

When the nineteenth century opened, the social scene under Bonaparte and his wife Josephine revived the glory and glamour of fine jewels. As the century progressed, engraved stones and cameos became "all the rage," adorning everything from madame's ears, fingers, neck, and tiara to the furniture in her salon. Once again, Gothic and Medieval designs gained favor, along with pieces more indicative of the Romantic Movement.

The importation of less valuable stones, such as amethyst, aquamarine, and topaz from Mexico and Brazil, made less expensive jewelry available, although still in gold settings. Diamonds were fea-

17

The invention of the electric light bulb late in the century affected innumerable areas of life and commerce, most of them far-reaching and of enormous future consequence. Surprisingly, the light bulb had a major effect on...of all things...jewelry! The brilliant light that emanated from the stones under this new, artificial light was at its most intense when refracted from diamonds, bouncing from their surface in a dazzling and impressive display. As a consequence, other precious stones took a "back seat" to their glittering rival.

In the nineteenth century, European mass-produced costume jewelry was generally considered to show little merit in either design or application, "...and it was against this tendency that the Art Nouveau artists raised their standards."[7] Inexpensive natural materials like ivory, jet, coral–even amethysts and garnets– were incorporated into jewelry designs with meritorious results.

Prior to that time, however, some Victorian jewelry had become tarred with an often undeserved reputation for including what were then considered relatively worthless stones. As a consequence, many pieces were "dismantled" or sold outright, frequently with unfortunate results, such as assuming that what were actually rubies were instead garnets. The predetermination that the cost of stones was the only point of value, thereby undercutting the aesthetic value of many fine designs, was a misnomer. Nevertheless, although a wealth of exceptional Victorian pieces were undoubtedly lost, many can still be enjoyed today.

Here too was a century that brought athleticism into jewelry design. Women gained more freedom, and jewelry reflected the sudden participation in physical activity by both sexes. Not unlike today, such activities as tennis and equestrianism fostered all manner of interesting jewelry designs featuring horses, hunting dogs (and accoutrements like saddles and hunting horns) along with bicycles and tennis rackets.

By the end of the nineteenth century, the art of jewelry-making had become *d'rigeur* in loosely related but nevertheless unexpected fields. In fact, "...nearly every artist and decorator made jewelry at the end of the century...it must be stressed that these pieces are far more than costume jewelry, even though they were made or distributed by recognized jewelry firms...They are sometimes criticized as being *objets d'art* or show pieces rather than jewelry–this criticism was even leveled at Lalique–but it cannot be denied that they were ultimately accepted and that they contributed substantially to the formation of the early twentieth century style."[8]

It is interesting to note how closely upscale costume jewelry of the twentieth century reflects the designs of fine jewelry of the preceding four centuries.

A long wing pearl and genuine ruby, 1" x .5".

In many instances, they appear almost interchangeable. Comparisons to the pieces of the eighteenth century are especially remarkable in their resemblance to elaborate costume designs that gained favor during the twentieth century's "golden age" of the costume jewelers' art.

Champleve enamel and a wing pearl; size 1" x .75".

This brooch, measuring 1.5" x .5" and marked 14K, has a baroque pearl, genuine seed pearl, and a champleve leaf.

A rose-cut diamond graces this stylized Art Nouveau leaf, this time in 14K gold and champleve enameling.

Three genuine wing pearls intertwine this tiny circular pin, measuring just .75".

A large genuine wing pearl sits regally atop a champleve flower on this Art Nouveau bar pin.

An orchid for milady? Of the same genre, but in a slightly larger design, this 1.5" brooch features a precious orchid and genuine baroque pearl.

Three rose-cut diamonds and a tiny baroque pearl, 1.25" x 1".

Worthy of being placed on a pedestal, these charming pins represent the winning combination of brass with gems, pearls, and enameling that was popular during the Art Nouveau period and often graced the neck of Gibson girl blouses. All are fine examples of the graceful lines of Art Nouveau design and the elegant quality that was added when combined with brass. It should be noted that the wing pearls featured in several of these are of a shape that is rarely seen and contributes to their value. These pieces have become very popular and the category is highly collectible. Making it doubly intriguing is the fact that it's virtually impossible to discern with the naked eye the difference between the brass and 14K gold pins, some of which can be found with Tiffany markings. The costume pieces employed the same designs, using genuine stones and pearls, with the brass glowing like burnished gold.

This design with graceful leaves has a tiny baroque pearl in center.

When the calla lilies are in bloom...1.75" x .75", with a baroque pearl.

Brass and Glass

"Brass and glass" has become an independent collecting field for many today, offering an exciting combination of materials often used in the fashioning of antique jewelry, purses, and feminine boudoir items. Rising to popularity during the Victorian era, its influence is often found in today's contemporary jewelry. This category offers seemingly endless variations of color, size, shape, texture, design, and even weight. The skilled workmanship to be found in brass and glass of this period was most often the result of the uncompromising tenets of European guild craftsmanship.

Two hundred and twenty scalloped, interlocking brass caps in four graduated colorations are strung on a metal chain, dramatically offsetting a faux carnelian-centered pendant.

In the Art Deco tradition, a faux amethyst pendant, offset by muted jade inserts and enameling.

A brilliant display of color...jeweled necklace with ornate incorporated chain. Circa 1930.

Fine example of Victorian filigree work, this one with elaborate tassel detail and faux amethyst stones. Its companion features brilliant blues.

From the Art Deco period, three colorful brooches; note the delicate enameling on the piece to the left.

This brass and glass necklace has the look of ancient Egypt, with its brass sections ornately detailed with sparkling stones and overlaid filigree designs.

Regal...from the Art Deco period but with much of the elaborate design style to be found in the Victorian era, a bezel-set brooch of brilliant stones and chain detail.

All brass and glass jewelry courtesy of Jeanne Graf Roberts.

Circa 1900-1910, a trio of sash pins, all with high relief, fancy metalwork, and brilliantly faceted stones.

Art Nouveau to Art Deco and Beyond

A revolution in jewelry design emerged in 1895 and continued until about 1910. Known as Art Nouveau, it was the first important movement of the twentieth century and captured the public's imagination more forcefully than any had before. Art Nouveau style glorified femininity in a fanciful, romantic way yet in many respects it was decidedly unconventional, replete with sensuous figurals, flowing hair, fairies, butterflies, and all manner of winged insects. An interim "transitional" period followed, which served as a bridge between the Art Nouveau and Art Deco movements.

At first, the dominant medium for decoration most indicative of Art Nouveau style was colored enameling. Gradually, enamel decoration lost its appeal in favor of the addition of stones to the designs. These were usually not cut gemstones, but rather natural stones of far less value like malachite, onyx, and agates, all of which epitomized the naturalism of the new style. The use of more humble materials "...was a reaction against the age-old conventions which too often led the nineteenth century bourgeoisie to mistake market value for aesthetic quality. An object is not necessarily beautiful because it costs a lot, and this was what these artists wanted to prove."[9] Art Nouveau was indeed "the start of something big" in the evolution of jewelry and had a dramatic impact on the status of costume jewelry that was to follow. Indeed, a new era was at long last dawning on the "jewelry horizon."

High regard for craftsmanship, rather than the mere cost of the components, led the public to gradually want to identify the jewelry makers. The maker's signature became an important part of jewelry's identity and desirability. Hence, the Art Nouveau movement provided opportunity for an artist to attain both individual self-expression and recognition. The result was far-reaching, encouraging creative people who would probably not otherwise have ventured into the field to become jewelers. The repercussions would have a major impact on jewelry from that time forward.

It is interesting to note that "Another characteristic of this period was the way sculptors and painters participated in the minor arts...during the Renaissance, many goldsmiths became painters. In the late nineteenth century, the reverse is true."[10] It is a trend that continues, quite successfully, and to the decided benefit of the jewelry industry, these many years later. In some respects, this could be referred to as an upscale crafts movement, for it resulted in individuals who specialized in art works of a more expensive nature selling "art jewelry." "It could be said that nearly every artist and decorator made jewelry at the end of the 19th century."[11] Since the living environment was strongly influenced by a seemingly unrelated artistic movement, the role of many decorators and artists became mutually intertwined.

Art Nouveau style enjoyed worldwide popularity, with much of it being designed and produced in Germany and Austria, where it was called *Jugendstil* or *Sezession*. However, the pieces were of a more commercial nature, which necessitated quantity production methods. German Art Nouveau was more angular and sharp edged, for "...the great German pioneers of international modern architecture (like)...Walter Gropius...killed the curve almost before it had appeared there."[12]

In direct contrast were designs emanating from France and Belgium, with lines clinging to the curve and in softer focus, which was reflected in the work of the French genius René Lalique. His jewelry, which often drew inspiration from Japan, was replete with engraved glass of unparalleled beauty that was frequently enhanced with amber and precious stones. In 1895, he was the paramount influence in introducing the nude female figure into jewelry. His displays of Art Nouveau designs at the Paris Centennial Exhibition of 1900 created a furor of interest in the movement and also influenced clothing fashions in the Art Nouveau tradition. Lalique continued with jewelry design until 1914, when he decided to devote most of his attention to glass objects. His fellow Frenchman Georges Fouquet also designed pieces of high quality and style similar to Lalique's, as did Paul Henri Vever, of the French house by that name, with both responsible for trend-setting jewelry that integrated the finest applications of the Art Nouveau movement. In Belgium, the sculptor Phillipe Wolfers–although working in the medium for only a few short years–created jewelry with marvelous technique and design, incorporating enameling, pearls, and precious and semi-precious stones.

Any discussion of Art Nouveau jewelry, costume or precious, would be sorely lacking without mention of the glory to be found in the works of Carl Fabergé and his son Peter Carl Fabergé. A Fabergé Art Nouveau pendant is described thus: "Shaped as a branch with three leaves covered in gold-green translucent enamel, with three circular diamonds suspended on stalks."[13] A masterpiece in the true sense of the word, his work set a standard of design in heights most mortals could but strive to attain. Unfortunately, although Fabergé considered himself foremost a jeweler, little remains for today's artisans to learn from, in either fine or upscale costume design, for: "Of the lavish pearl and diamond necklaces mentioned in accounts...none seems to have survived the decimation of war..."[14], and examples of smaller pieces are most often seen now only in workshop sketchbooks.

In Britain, according to Britisher Graham Hughes, "...Art Nouveau was almost stillborn because of British reticence; as a nation we do not indulge in orgies of visual fun."[15] Denmark, on the other hand, gave the Art Nouveau movement tremendous impetus with the distinctive artistry of Georg Jensen, who chose to interpret the movement with a style that carried it into still other dimensions, his work being generally heavier in appearance and deviating from curvy and more elaborate designs, thus forming the basis for the modernistic jewelry of the 1930s.

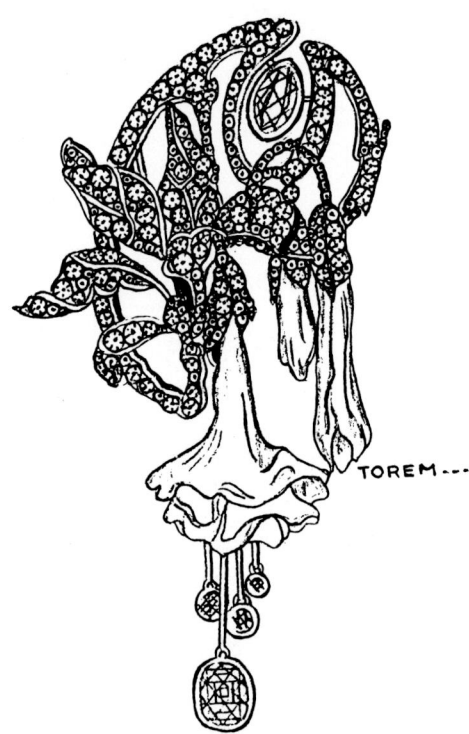

For the Paris Exposition of 1904, this design (*Falquieres Pendéntifs, Broches*) epitomizes the essence of the Art Nouveau movement.

As with all other revolutionary movements, it was inevitable that the Art Nouveau style would come to an end. As the social, political, and economic conditions of the world changed, so too did women's fashion and jewelry. Graham Hughes observed, "Art Nouveau was a crazy but exciting reaction against convention; against big stones, big money, boring colours and conventional dress." Instead, "It was obsessed with endless creepers and leaves, dream-sodden faces, soft, irregular low relief, dusky colours....But in the end...its own exaggerations killed it."[16]

Many of the Art Nouveau styles formed the design basis for much of the costume jewelry that was to follow. For example, the delicate glass flowers often found in Art Nouveau designs had their own counterparts in costume, as did many fine enameled pieces. The bees and butterflies of Art Nouveau were resurrected at mid-century and beyond, along with the reptile and beetle themes of Art Deco. Also making their way–with much success–into the 20th century were ancient concepts employing figures like Etruscan ram's heads, all manner of wild beasts, snakes, alligators, mythological creatures, and even fire-breathing dragons. All of these remain a vital part of today's jewelry, as modern designers offer their own versions of old favorites.

Following the somewhat hazy "transitional" period, Art Deco burst on the scene. Its beauty took many forms, but "...it is in the field of jewellery that Art Deco reaches the very zenith of its stylishness."[17] Clothing fashion, as always, played a major role in jewelry styles of the period, one which emphasized the female form in silhouettes that "cried out" for long beads, swinging in a carefree style that reflected the new-found freedom of the wearer. "For daytime, the clutter of bracelets was replaced by jangling bangles of ivory or jade, real or artificial, and an essential accessory for the 'flapper'...was the ivory bangle, sometimes paste-studded, worn just above the elbow, with a chiffon handkerchief tucked into it"[18] (which explains why so many attractive bangles from yesteryear fall off our wrists –they weren't intended to be worn there in the first place!).

One of Faberge's Deco style necklaces had fifteen links, was made of platinum set with rose diamonds and ice crystal motifs and separated into two bracelets...an innovation later used with much success on costume pieces. Often lush and replete with magnificent faux stones, they sometimes separated into two and even three parts (e.g., necklace and bracelet combinations, one brooch or dual clips, and even pieces that could be converted singly to a necklace, bracelet, and brooch). Also innovative at this time were "night and day" brooches with petaled flowers that opened and closed, and even reversible pieces with an ingenious revolving pinback arrangement, to display one side for day and the other for night.

The most popular of these interchangeable designs was the "dual clip." Here was an example of jewelry design forcefully adapting to the fashions of the time and in the process, creating an exciting jeweled accessory that was "ex-

Two 1900s designs by René Lalique.

actly right." The dual clip appeared at first glance to be a single-piece brooch but could be transformed into two separate clips, each complementary to the other (and especially appropriate for "sweetheart" dress necklines so popular in the 1930s). It was two (even three) pieces for the price of one, and the public loved it. Initially designed by major jewelers in precious metals and replete with precious and semi-precious stones, they were copied for the general market in common materials geared to make them accessible to everyone.

There was an elegance in the sleek, clean lines of Art Deco jewelry. The designs, with their unusual combinations of materials, were striking and unique. "People who are accustomed to evaluating diamonds by their cut, color, and clarity are baffled when assessing a Deco piece, in which the quality of the diamond is secondary to the artistry and workmanship of the entire piece."[19] The enthusiastic acceptance of this unexpected marriage of materials and designs taking precedence over the value of the stones made the Art Deco period well-suited to combining "paste" jewels with non-precious metals and unusual materials. Even pencil and gouache designs from a Fabergé album show Art Deco brooches which reflect a mix of materials that "trickled down" to costume pieces of the era.

Coupled with the genius of its Art Nouveau predecessors, the Art Deco movement became a benchmark in the evolution of costume jewelry. Hundreds of companies devoted to its design and production were established, catapulting the industry to its much-deserved apex. Many artists and craftsmen had struggled long and hard to achieve recognition for their work. Both individually and as a group, they would finally earn a respected niche in the jewelry world.

A 1914 design by Weirner Werkstatte.

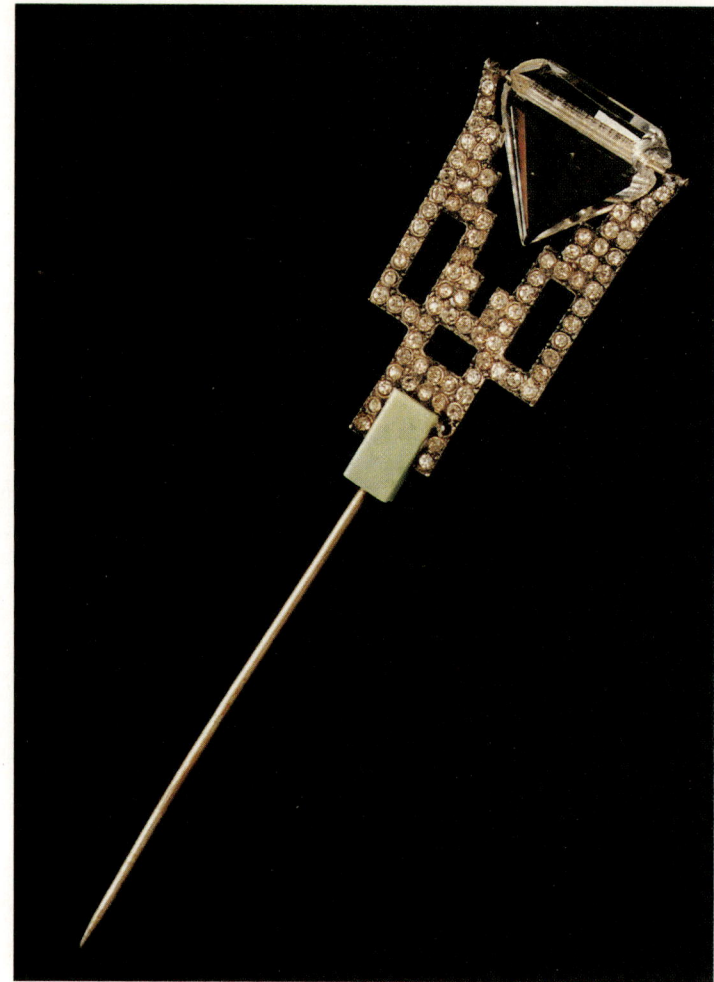

This 2.5" French Art Deco stickpin has a clear glass rotating section and a jade base.

Four unsigned, or jewelry store initialed, bracelets, all reflecting the ambiance of the Art Deco period.

These cruise ship illustrations are from a 1934 promotional folder.

From the Art Deco period, a pearl bracelet with elaborate clasp.

An early Tecla Pearl ad.

From the 1920s, these fabulous pieces pay silent tribute to the patience required to produce fine mosaics...and the beauty that results.

This unsigned piece has a leaded back and a Victorian look yet is also in the genre of fine jewelry from the Art Deco period. Here is an example from that movement, emphasizing the design, with the stones merely complementary to its beauty.

The Couture Connection

Couture fashions had a significant and positive influence in this evolution. The designs of Paul Poiret provided fertile ground for "costume" jewelry, and he is acknowledged as the "...first couturier to consider using it in his collection. Commissioning the Parisian jewelers René Boivin and Gripoix, and the artist Paul Iribe, he accessorized his clothes with tassel-style jewelry."[20] The artistry of Gripoix made its way into Poiret's salon in a somewhat unexpected way, for he and his wife created a special aquarium mixing the authentic with the imaginary; real fish intermingled with sparkling glass ones in what must have been a dazzling display!

It took a pair of international fashion mavens, however, to further assist this relatively new endeavor along the bumpy road to respectability in the mid-twentieth century. "Coco" Chanel and Elsa Schiaparelli were at the forefront of the movement to provide accessories in a "lighter vein." Chanel recognized early on that "costume" jewelry was for all women, including the wealthy, who had previously shunned it, and offered delightful alternatives to the rigidity of the past. Schiaparelli's style was particularly playful, introducing all manner of accessory items that would be considered outrageous (but oh, so charming!) even today, veering far afield from the simplistic beauty of Art Deco to one more apt to bring a smile to the face! Both helped to create the image of the "roaring Twenties" as a daring, devil-may-care one. In light of the somewhat prudish times that preceded it, that illustrious decade became a bellwether for much that followed in female attitudes and social demands...all of which, both directly and indirectly, affected fashion. Chanel and Schiaparelli had been major players in designing haute couture garments for women of this new era, and wisely deduced that accessorizing was paramount to establishing a "complete fashion picture." Costume jewelry was an essential component of this picture and each was "off and running," along with other up and coming "giants" in the field. The popularity of costume jewelry was like a roller coaster ride that would stay on the fast track for several decades, diminish for a short period in the 1970s and early Eighties, and then pick itself up, dust itself off, and proceed full steam ahead into the remaining years of the Eighties and the century's final decade.

1 Hughes, *The Art of Jewelry*, p. 233
2 Sterling Publishing, *Gemstones*, p. 46
3 Hughes, *The Art of Jewelry*, p. 19
4 Lanllier and Pini, *Five Centuries of Jewelry*, p. 81
5 Ibid., p. 98
6 Ibid., p. 122
7 Ibid., p. 162
8 Ibid., p. 214
9 Ibid., p. 199
10 Ibid., p. 216
11 Ibid., p. 214
12 Hughes, *The Art of Jewelry*, p. 110
13 Faberge Arts Foundation, *Faberge: Imperial Jeweller*, p. 350
14 Ibid., p. 359
15 Hughes, *The Art of Jewelry*, p. 109
16 Ibid., p. 104
17 Van de Lemme, *A Guide to Art Deco Style*, p. 118
18 Becker, *Fabulous Costume Jewelry*, p. 123
19 Adams, *Traditional Home*, p. 111
20 Mulvagh, *Costume Jewelry in Vogue*, p. 36

Early 1920s French paste brooch rests comfortably on a fashion drawing by LePape, from a 1920 *Le Gazette du Bon Ton*.

The Techniques and Process

An examination of the jewelry-making process would encompass volumes, for it involves countless techniques. Every element of each piece is complex, with each step depending upon the skills and knowledge of many people with a wealth of individual talents. What is taken for granted by the layman is the result of complex procedures involving hours of difficult work. Beyond the element of individual expression, the process of artistic endeavors creates an object that appeals to the senses of the viewers individually. Display a dozen dissimilar items in the same general category together and it is inevitable that each will attract its own coterie of admirers, whether it be a painting, an evening gown...or a jeweled bauble to hang around one's neck! It is this variety of tastes and proclivities that propels the artist to new heights of innovation, and encourages him or her to take that giant leap beyond the norm.

From earliest times, elements in jewelry-making were diverse. For example, jewelry made of iron enjoyed popularity in the period of Classicism and the Gothic style, and was even particularly popular in the early and mid-nineteenth century. To find jewelry artisans in the environment of an iron foundry may at first seem incongruous, but some of the finest designers of the period worked there. In fact, those who crafted most effectively in iron had initially been trained as goldsmiths. "Karl Friedrich Schinkel (1781-1841)...worked for the Berlin foundries. Schinkel was celebrated for a charming neo-Gothic style, which lent itself particularly well to Berlin iron jewellery..."[1] While jewelry made of iron was most often associated with German designers, artisans in this medium, such as Simion Pierre Devarrone, also flourished in France. Even Monsieur Caque, an engraver for the Paris Mint, was proficient in making iron jewelry, which reached a peak of popularity when Prussia liberated itself from Napoleon's yoke of oppression in 1813. "In order to raise funds for arms, patriotic Prussian women gave up their gold jewellery, including wedding rings, and received in exchange reproductions of their gifts, inscribed or with a certificate stating *'Gold Gab ich fur Eisen'*–I gave gold for iron."[2]

Rings of iron had been common ornaments many centuries before. In early Roman times, women wore gold wedding rings in public but in the confines of their homes they donned plain circlets of unset iron. During the 19th and even into the 20th century, rings of iron remained in favor especially in Germany, where many were used as wedding rings. The inevitable problem of rust stains was finally solved during the early years of the 20th century when a thin layer of gold was added to the inside. During the First World War, a significant amount of melted gold from rings was donated for the war effort by patriotic Germans, just as they had done a hundred years before. The French and Italians also gave up their jewelry to raise money for their countries. These wartime sacrifices gave impetus to a popular trend to concentrate less on fine jewelry and more on alternative decorative accents.

Whether of gold or iron, or whatever the complex technique, when dealing with quality every step of the jewelry-making process must be handled with patience and care. From the initial design, through carving, modeling, and casting, each of these steps requires complex equipment and intricate skills.

There is a universal truth in the preface of Alexander Fisher's 1906 book entitled *The Art of Enamelling Upon Metal*:
"I have kept the technical descriptions of processes as brief as is compatible with clearness. Other methods I have been compelled to omit, owing to the intricacy and complexity involved in their

manufacture. *These cannot be explained except and save by the aid of demonstration, and even then can only be really understood and appreciated after some years of study and practice."*

In the same spirit, brief synopses of some of the techniques involved in the production of jewelry–both fine and costume–are outlined below. *They have been chosen to provide a cursory insight into the complexities of jewelry-making, and are representative of countless techniques covering many areas of expertise.* The photographic examples to follow can then be appreciated for the complexity of workmanship and infinite patience each represents.

Enameling

"There is a fascination about the alchemy of metal, glass, and fire that is inescapable." [3]

Indeed, enameling offers enormous possibilities for self expression, not only in jewelry-making, but many other artistic endeavors. It is the technique that "gave birth" to more advanced forms of this application, like cloisonné, champlevé, and plique-à-jour, most requiring a combination of natural components–a metal (most usually copper, but silver and gold have also been used quite effectively) and glass. Along with plique-à-jour and cloisonné, enameling played an integral part in the Art Nouveau movement, where the first tentative steps were made that eventually led to what would later be known as "costume" jewelry.

Simply stated, for an application that far surpasses "simple," the enameling process requires first an acid bath to thoroughly cleanse the metal, powdered enamel–and, for the more advanced, a pre-cleansing of the powdered enamels––and a kiln. Replete with necessities such as nitric acid, carborundum stones, spreaders, scrolling tools, and adhesives, enameling is a technique whereby a piece of metal is covered with a thin layer of adhesive, over which powdered enamel is sifted. The piece is then dried, placed on a rack, and baked in a kiln. During this process the powdered enamel slowly liquifies. First one side is done, then the other, with imperfections any time along the way smoothed off, corrected, and rebaked. Called counterenameling, it precedes the actual enameling process, which involves once again applying a thin layer of adhesive, followed by the enamel, and proceeding with the same kiln process, however this time placing the piece on a trivet and then a mesh rack. Each successive firing enhances the glossy finish so appealing in enamel pieces.

Birds of a feather...with old lead backs, these enameled fur clips from the 1920s or Thirties soar to new heights of style and charm.

This is only the beginning, however, for when the initial steps are completed, a design is then applied, first by dipping the brush sparingly into adhesive and drawing the design of one's choice. The chosen color is sifted over the entire piece, and it is then turned, allowing any particles not on the adhesive surface to fall free. Even stencil forms can be used once the process reaches this stage. Now comes the time for artists to exercise their own concepts, which can include techniques such as "lumping," "threading," and "swirling," all capable of adding a three-dimensional, sometimes confetti-like effect to the final image. The entire process is a tedious exercise in patience, with one color being applied for each firing, but the result is well worth the wait for those with the resolve to undertake it.

"Jewels" (often simply pieces of interesting and colorful glass) can quite effectively be added to enameled pieces. This is accomplished in several ways. One is by placing the stone on the powdered enamel as it is being prepared for the first firing in the hope that it will secure as it sinks into the melting enamel. More popular, and with less potential for mishaps, is to place the jeweled pieces on the base-coat enamel with adhesive after the underfiring has taken place. This step is followed by the second firing. Here too the stone sinks into position as the enamel is brought to its "glassy" stage.

Enameling did not exert its independence as a separate and distinct art form until the 12th century, for in the earlier enameling processes it was "...employed from a goldsmith's or jeweler's point of view, not from that of a genuine worker in enamel. It is not till we come to the twelfth century that the fine craft of enamelling begins to assert its independence as an art and its full capacity for change and progress. From that time onward we meet with enamel done per se."[4]

Such diverse cultures as those found in the Byzantine and Ireland were long acknowledged centers of learning, "...and in art they were unrivaled for the beauty of their enamels in cloisonné and champlevé...in form, in drawing, to be sure, there is a lack of the symmetry and grace that we find in the intaglio of the early Etruscans, but the work had a form, an expression, a magic, peculiarly right in champlevé enamelling. The graduated colouring between the metal lines, the tones of the whites, the yellows, and, indeed of all the colours, are as beautiful as Persian tiles or as plates of Damascus."[5]

The 18th century ushered in the "rococo" period, which lent its own expression to enameling. As an example of how involved this work could become, a description of the steps necessary to execute an enameled piece, to satisfy the "rococo" environment, is described thus: "First a figure was carved, then either immersed or painted so that only its face and head, for instance, would be gold metal, all the clothes being enamel; it was an amazing feat to make the molten glass stay in place on its various planes especially as each colour had a different melting point and therefore needed its separate firing."[6]

The name Fabergé inspires awe for his genius in many art forms, but in none does it signify the epitome of craftsmanship more readily than in the enameling process. "The most sought after objects from Fabergé have been those crafted in gold or silver and covered with delicately coloured coats of enamel applied over cunning engine-turned backgrounds. It was Fabergé's re-invention and perfection of the complicated technique of translucent enamel that brought him the highest praise..."[7] In describing the coats of enamel applied to Faberge's guillache of engine turning, "...A last coat of fondant, or transparent enamel, was lovingly polished for hours on a wooden wheel and buffed to give the object its unique gloss."[8]

Champlevé

Also employing the enameling process, *champlevé* is derived from the French words "champ" (a field) and "leve" (raised), along with basse taille, which was perfected by Western enamelers in France and the Byzantine. This technique involves etching the metals into channels, which is time-consuming to be sure, but far less than the hours of painstaking chiseling necessary to perfect this procedure hundreds of years earlier. This etching process creates an insertion of color in the metal, which can be copper, silver, or gold. The piece is then covered with asphalt paint and dried. Dividing lines are chosen, i.e., those areas covered with paint will remain with the bright metal finish, and the sketch applied will be etched away by the acid. Asphalt paint is again applied to these lines, divided into design areas, dried thoroughly, and placed in an etched bath. When ready, the piece is rinsed and the asphalt paint removed with turpentine and a soft cloth. The counter-enameling process then begins, with wet enamel carefully placed and built-up in the etched depressions, and fired as before.

Basse-Taille

Reaching its height of popularity in the 14th century, an offshoot of champlevé is *basse taille*, taken from the French "basse" meaning low and "taille" meaning cut, thus low cut or bas-relief. Perfected by Western enamelers in France and the Byzantine, this technique involves a complex combination of metal working and enameling skills. Working first in metal, a bas relief design is raised, requiring advanced knowledge of numerous tools of the metal-workers' art. After cleansing, transparent enamel is then carefully applied in layers until the exact shading desired is achieved. Because of the bas relief and detailed metal de-

Flights of fancy...of French origin, marked "sterling" and "champleve," this winged creature is a fine example of the technique.

signs, a three dimensional effect is created when heavier deposits of enamel build up in the deeper crevices. In this instance, when the enamel is placed over the surface, the relief portion appears through the transparent enamel, giving a stained glass effect, but often with the added beauty of sculptures in low relief decorating the metal behind.

causing the enamel to become liquid and the wires to sink into position. After removal and drying, individual colors are applied, dropping each into its respective enclosure, and the firing process begins again. It is usually necessary to repeat this tedious undertaking numerous times until all areas are smooth and defect free. When finally complete, the

Plique-à-jour

Plique-à-jour is best described as an application of the cloisonné technique minus the metal backing, creating a "window" effect whereby light transposes the colors from the back. It is a process in which "...the metal is not inlaid after the enamel object is made, but...is propor-

German made, these large sterling floral brooches are a colorful melange of enamel and pearls with Old World cut steel accents.

Cloissoné

In direct contrast to champlevé, *cloisonné* is a process whereby thin strips of wire are set in the hollows, with each color essentially "boxed into" its own enclosure. This laborious technique involves a succession of intricate processes. The wire is first coiled and kiln-baked to make it pliable, then bent into the pre-determined design in such a manner as to keep it upright during firing. The metal piece is again coated with adhesive, and the wires are, one by one, put into their proper place in the design, making certain that all corners merge. Once again, the piece is fired,

piece is held under water while a carborundum stone smoothes the entire surface, resulting in a matte finish that is often desirable in the artist's concept of the piece. If a more glossy surface is needed, however, it must return to the kiln yet again.

Under the best of circumstances, this is an exceedingly painstaking and lengthy procedure. Without the benefit of modern technology, the amount of time and effort involved to create the cloisonné pieces of centuries ago is a lesson in patience we would be hard-pressed to surpass today

tionately so far in excess of the metal that it is the reverse of the condition of the enamels."[9] This requires etching away the inside metal shell with acid after firing, with only the wires (in this case, somewhat heavier yet finer than in cloisonné) serving as the filigree-like supports. Each cavity is then filled with glass lumps and/or transparent enamels and quickly fired, after which the enamel springs miraculously free of the retaining wires. An art form most often associated with the Orient, plique-à-jour remains popular in many modes of design today, including vases, bowls, and lamps.

36

However, here too is a technique long favored in jewelry, where a play of color through light adds much to the appeal of the piece, such as in dangling earrings, medallions, and pendants. Thus, the translation of plique-à-jour becomes clear, for it literally means "open to daylight."

Repoussé

Repoussé is a form of embossing, similar to that of modeling with soft materials like wax. In this case, however, the metal itself is the material, involving placing it on a substance that will allow impressions to be made as the relief design takes shape. First a design is drawn or transferred onto the metal, following which it is placed on the substance chosen (like plaster or pitch), warmed, and then cooled. A small tool is employed to painstakingly trace each line of the design, a technique often requiring frequent striking with a special hammer-like instrument, thereby creating separate channels in the metal. By reversing the piece, each channel becomes raised, offering an infinite number of design possibilities, from seemingly simple flower petals to free-form modernistic ones. The piece is then warmed with a blowpipe to soften the pitch (or whatever), thereby enabling it to be removed. This entire process can be repeated as many times as necessary to improve the perfection of the piece. If stones are part of the design, bezels must then be made and soldered into place.

Some designs require chasing (such as for veins in the leaves of flowers), which creates yet another step in the technique. Chasing "...does not remove the metal, as in engraving, but tends to make it rise into slight ridges. Small repeat patterns are built up in this way..."[10] When all is complete, the open spaces are cut out and stones inserted.

1 Becker, *Fabulous Costume Jewelry*, p. 55
2 Robins, *An A-Z of Gems and Jewelry*, p. 48
3 Remenih, *Enameling*, p. 4
4 Fisher, *The Art of Enamelling Upon Metal*, p. 10
5 Ibid., pp. 10, 11
6 Hughes, *The Art of Jewelry*, p. 189
7 Faberge Arts Foundation, *Faberge: Imperial Jeweller*, p. 30
8 Ibid., p. 30
9 Fisher, *The Art of Enamelling Upon Metal*, p. 27
10 Robins, *An A-Z of Gems and Jewelry*, p. 24

Beads, beads, beads, in all sizes and shapes, from frosted, jewel-encrusted ones (like prickly raspberries!), to opaque nuggets, Victorian jets, and sparkling crystals.

A Gem of a Gem

"There are hundreds of minerals that possess the beauty and durability necessary to a gemstone ...stones considered precious today usually possess a combination in richness in color and real or artificial rarity."[1]

In earlier times the desirability of a stone was predicated on somewhat different standards, for often "...the most colorful stones that could be worked easily were of greatest value...As the skill of gem cutting--lapidary--developed, harder materials such as quartz, amethyst, ruby, sapphire and diamond were introduced."[2] On the other hand, artificially-induced rarity can be applied to diamonds, which have for years maintained a mystique of desirability among "precious" stones. Diamonds are, in fact, plentiful, but carefully controlled by cost.

What are generally referred to as precious stones are either clear or translucent, and facet-cut, to further enhance their beauty. Specific choices in this very limited category varied throughout history. Today, "Diamond, emerald, sapphire, ruby...are considered by most gemologists to be precious, while all other stones are considered semi-precious."[3] The term "gemstone" encompasses all of the above.

Referred to as "roughs," even raw gems which have been tumbled for hours and refined into shapes to resemble polished stones, much like those worn away for countless years by water, have successfully been used to create jewelry with a rich and unusual appeal.

Costume jewelry designers of this century have availed themselves of many semi-precious stones, with magnificent results. For the most part, however, their creations have had to employ "imitation" stones, a category that is both broad and rich in possibilities. Here we find the general appearance of natural stones, but with physical properties and composition of a much different nature. In one form or another, all lend themselves nicely to the wide variety of design possibilities in fashioning costume jewelry. Glass, of course, comes readily to mind, along with synthetic materials like plastics and lucite. Glass stones are generally referred to as "paste." Although the term French paste is most commonly used, the term is actually derived "...from Italian pasta or dough because in most cases imitations are cast under pressure in a mould to give them a faceted form before polishing."[4] The more lead in the glass, the more brilliant the stone. Bohemian glass stones were frequently backed by a coating of mercury amalgam, while some French paste had a shiny "net cap" backing. Glass jewelry was adversely affected in Europe by the devastating economic and political conditions of the 1930s, but the beauty of the stones enjoyed unlimited popularity during the ensuing decades of costume jewelry's "golden age."

One of the first operations to successfully manufacture artificial stones and market costume jewelry was Gablonz of Bohemia (Czechoslovakia) during the 1700s. They even supplied foreign markets with quartz, glass, and artificial stones. An "explosion" in glass cutting then took place from 1867 to 1869, and Gablonz even established a school geared to covering many of the related skills necessary for jewelry production.

The term "rhinestone" was derived from their place of origin, for these dazzling beauties were first produced from Alpine rock crystals at a factory in Germany's Rhine River area. Most modern-day rhinestones, however, are glass productions from Czechoslovakia, Austria, and Bavaria. At the high-end of the glass stones category is cubic zirconia, which is highly refractive and often difficult to distinguish by simple examination; however, sophisticated methods can readily detect their lower reflectivity and heat conductance.

In like manner, "French jet" is an all-encompassing term for black glass, whereas actual jet is fossilized driftwood generally found on the coast of Yorkshire. The struggling and tiny "jet" industry happily flourished when Queen Victoria decreed that only black jewelry was acceptable for wear following the death of her beloved Prince Albert. Much of the black glass production during that time was in Gablonz. "Its raw material was stone that had been pressed from black pyrolusite glass and then cut...it still ranks among the best costume jewelry that Gablonz manufacturers ever produced,"[5] and jet jewelry has remained popular in one form or another ever since.

In 1891, Daniel Swarovski received the first patent involving cutting rhinestones by mechanical means, and during the 20th century Swarovski has supplied glass stones from Austria. The color, clarity, and quality of Swarovski stones need little introduction. "Swarovski glass was initially produced in 22 colors, which subsequently became 51, and nowadays 67...In 1950, the Swarovski company was the only one in the industry able to produce the color 'golden fuschia'...very fashionable all over the world at that time."[6]

Many fine American bead and crystal houses flourished at mid-century and beyond. These included: Royal Bead, owned by Paul and Bill Detkin, which was responsible for the Laguna jewelry line and specialized in pearls; Deauville Beads, owned by Bob Kaplan, which specialized in the crystal beads that were especially popular during the 1950s and '60s; Clio Novelties, located in Brooklyn; and Imperial Pearl, which produced not only faux pearls but many of their own costume jewelry pieces.

Foiling, which involves backing a paler stone with reflective colored foil to make it appear brighter, is a common practice in costume jewelry. Ingenuity went beyond the use of colored paper or metal foil, however, for "...at one time it was common practice to 'foil' a pale blue sapphire by backing it with a blue section of a peacock's feather."[7] It should be emphasized that in striving to have all the stones in a given piece be of a matching color, skillful foiling is necessary, thereby enhancing not only the beauty of the piece but its value as well.

Composite stones have been made since Roman times, and their most common form is the doublet; e.g., two pieces of stone cemented together, sandwich-style. Some doublets have a glass base topped with a hard mineral. "Garnet-topped doublets are made to imitate gems of all colours, but the function between garnet and glass is often easy to see...Soude emeralds consist of a quartz crown pavilion between which is a layer of emerald green glass or gelatine."[8]

Synthetic gems are another story altogether and outside the bounds of this work. They involve fusing the chemical compounds of the real stone in powder form, and are generally very fine copies of their original counterparts. These are man-made, usually under rigid laboratory conditions, where a series of complex steps are involved, including the melting of the appropriate coloring agents and minerals until they reach a specific crystallization stage. The result is a faux gem that appears startlingly close to the "real" thing. "The earliest gem-quality synthetics were the rubies produced in 1902 by Auguste Verneuil, using a flame fusion process."[9] Some synthetic gems require more expertise and time than others. Chief among these are emeralds, which can take as long as nine months to crystallize properly. In general, however, although capable of reproduction of good clarity and size, synthetic stones are more brittle. Nevertheless, they have the constituencies of their real counterparts and require considerable expense and expertise to perfect.

Not an "imitation" at all, marcasite, which falls into the shiny "gem" category, is a very appealing component of many jewelry designs from early in the century, most especially in Victorian and Art Deco styles. Later used with much success by top-quality vintage costume jewelry designers, marcasite's popularity has spawned a plethora of current reproductions that can easily be confused with vintage pieces. A close look at the older pieces of good quality makes the new ones easy to spot, for their workmanship is often shoddy. The stones and backings are also shinier and lack the "antique" look that makes the vintage styles so charming. This is not to denigrate the many attractive pieces of new marcasite jewelry available in today's market, but simply to caution the buyer to be aware that some marcasite pieces are not old.

Also apt to cause confusion is the difference between cut steel and marcasite, as many individuals randomly interchange the two terms. Cut steel is a shiny bit of bumpy metal, whereas marcasite is a crystallized material from the pyrite family, found in tones ranging from clear to unusual pale yellow and coppery shades, the latter two the result of the use of innovative goldplating in some vintage pieces of costume jewelry featuring marcasites. Generally intended for daytime wear, many inexpensive early cut-steel examples like turn-of-the-century shoe clips, buckles, and brooches, are not without their own distinctive charm. The subtle glitter of marcasites, on the other hand, was deemed more appropriate for evening. It is prudent to become familiar with both.

1 Von Neumann, *The Design and Creation of Jewelry*, p. 164
2 Von Neumann, Ibid., p. 7
3 Von Neumann, Ibid., p. 164
4 Robins, *An A-Z of Gems and Jewelry*, p. 63
5 Cera, *Jewels of Fantasy*, p. 372
6 Cera, Ibid, p. 377
6 Robins, *An A-Z of Gems and Jewelry*, p. 38
7 Sterling Publishing, *Gemstones*, p. 46
8 Ibid., p. 47
9 Ibid., p.47

The Factory and Workshop

The Tools

As with so many other outwardly genteel and high-end industries, what you see may be what you get...but what you don't see could easily "take the bloom off the rose." Although showcases glittering with baubles would belie what occurs behind the scenes, jewelry doesn't just "happen." The industry is fraught with problems and roadblocks, each of which must be solved before any process can proceed to the next level. Consumers, thankfully, needn't bother themselves with the so-called "dirty work," and that's as it should be; but those who are responsible for creating the end result from "day one" of the process would take a far different view. Everything is far from glamorous in the jewelry business. Here one finds tools that resemble those on carpenters' and handymen's benches in shops all over the world, such as saws, files, vises, shears, nippers, drill bits, and burs.

There are even templates, much like those used for art work and other office applications. In this case, however, they require many pieces of machinery capable of pressing hundreds of separate, individually-sized indentations into the metal stampings so necessary in most designs. With one template for each size or shape necessary, this could, again, become a very complex and lengthy operation, requiring a very specialized skill. To illustrate the complexity of this procedure, at least six or seven template operations are necessary to make a beaded piece, face it, and then press it into the brass. Another complication emerges in this scenario; because of the detail involved in layered sections, filigree designs become very difficult when working in the white metal most frequently used in costume pieces. On the other hand, by utilizing sterling or brass the problem is eliminated. The equipment necessary for all these operations requires a huge investment, with specialized companies often servicing much of the industry. Today their use has rapidly become a dying art.

The Metals and Plating Process

Costume jewelry, especially when being produced for the mass market, is generally manufactured by employing alloys, which are a combination of metals such as silver, copper, pewter, or other white metals. Consequently, plating is an important process in the manufacture of most costume jewelry. Since the pieces usually involve the use of base metals, they must be finished with a plated metal of a more precious nature. In electroplating, electrolysis is used. This generally involves a layer of copper, followed by nickel or chromium, and then a precious metal like gold or rhodium. When given a dull finish, or satinized, the piece must be brushed with matting powder.

Many higher-end designs are of sterling, which can, of course, remain in its finished "silver" state or undergo a goldplating process, resulting in what is referred to as vermeil.

Molds, Castings, Findings and Fittings

The business of molds and castings is but one example of the complexity of this multi-faceted industry. The techniques of jewelry castings (basically that of pouring molten metal into a mold) were developed thousands of years ago. Before the metal can be poured, a wax model must be made and then placed in the casting, "...with an opening through which it could be melted out and into which the molten metal could be poured. This is the almost universal cireperdue or lost wax process."[1] As time progressed, centrifugal pressure made it possible to rapidly propel the metal into the mold, and by the 1920s this method, first used in the dental industry, was also found to be amply suitable to the needs of the rapidly expanding costume jewelry business. Obviously, during the casting process the metal used must be able to convert to a liquid when heated, and modern techniques and advancements allow this to be done in spin casting facilities that are electrically driven.

Investment casting is a process requiring complex equipment, with its composition generally consisting of plastic, silica, boric acid, and graphite, which forms a hard substance that adheres tightly to the model. There are inherent problems, however, for "It must be porous enough to allow gases to escape before the incoming molten metal...plaster of paris alone will not withstand the heat requirements of an investment."[2] It must be noted, however, that the revolutionary acceptance of costume jewelry in the 20th century would not have occurred with such force without the casting procedure, for it "...revolutionized costume jewelry production in the 1930s. It is specifically geared to mass production and enabled manufacturers...to considerably reduce the cost of labor and materials."[3]

Every aspect of a piece of jewelry must be fashioned somewhere by someone. For example, the manufacture of fastenings is a separate industry, with its own designers and individuality. There are snap fasteners and swivels, simple

Design drawings from a 19th century German findings book.

yet appealing bar and toggle closings, threaded screws, box snaps, and bolt rings, with each playing an important but generally unheralded role in the "ins and outs" of the costume jewelry industry. Additionally, there are "findings"–again, an industry apart. These include the pin backs, jump rings, ear screws, wires, and safety chains. "...Of little artistic merit they are machine made, mass produced, and commercially available in gold, silver and base metals."[4] When created by hand for specific pieces, findings are often referred to as "fittings." Jewelry made simply from mass-produced findings differs greatly from that necessitating individual hand-crafted molds or fittings, which make their way into the higher-end costume jewelry market and are generally produced under the aegis of individual artists and craftsmen. Examining pieces of costume jewelry will readily ascertain that even seemingly simple components like wire can be an important element in the crafting of a piece. In the jewelry business, wire is not simply "wire," for it comes in all sizes and configurations, with some like the plaiting effect found in little girls' pigtails!

Not surprisingly, many highly-regarded companies involved in these operations are or were located in Europe, and it is from this core of artisans that the United States drew its own coterie of skilled craftsmen. They still exist in Paris today, for, "Around the Place de la Republique tiny Dickensian sweatshops create intricate and limited edition pieces for the grand couture houses."[5] During the 1950s, Winter, who also supplied many of the French couture houses, "...employed sixty craftsmen, each specializing in woodwork, metalwork or stone cutting...these craftsmen did not work in isolation but consulted the couturiers at the beginning of each season to determine a decorative theme..."[6] Another company, Janvier–founded in 1886–remains a repository for a plethora of findings, numbering in excess of 150,000, many of which contemporary jewelry designers eagerly incorporate into today's designs.

Foundries and jewelry may seem diametrically opposed and rarely thought of as "companions" (at least not since the days of Berlin Iron jewelry), but the "marriage" Joan Castle Joseff and her late husband Eugene Joseff, better known as Joseff of Hollywood, melded between investment casting and glittering jewels of the "silver screen" is a prime example of how investment cast jewelry can successfully be intertwined with aerospace parts. During World War II it was found that jewelry-making processes, as well as the factories in which these processes took place, were admirably suited for conversion to defense projects. Thus, many jewelry firms suddenly found themselves caught up in the war effort in a most unexpected way.

There were other repercussions, as well. For instance, in the case of Joseff of Hollywood, what began as the production of small airplane parts during the war became a full-time endeavor at war's end, with airplane parts by Joseff flying on almost every commercial airliner since. Hence, the unexpected interaction between the metal parts that fly in the sky and the costume jewelry bird that elegantly soars on our lapel!

1 Von Neumann, *The Design and Creation of Jewelry*, p. 93
2 Ibid, pp. 97, 98
3 Cera, *Jewels of Fantasy*, p. 390
4 Robins, *An A-Z of Gems and Jewelry*, p. 37
5 Mulvagh, *Costume Jewelry in Vogue*, p. 18
6 Ibid, p. 99

Possibly a student's exercise book, these drawings are from a 1907 European journal.

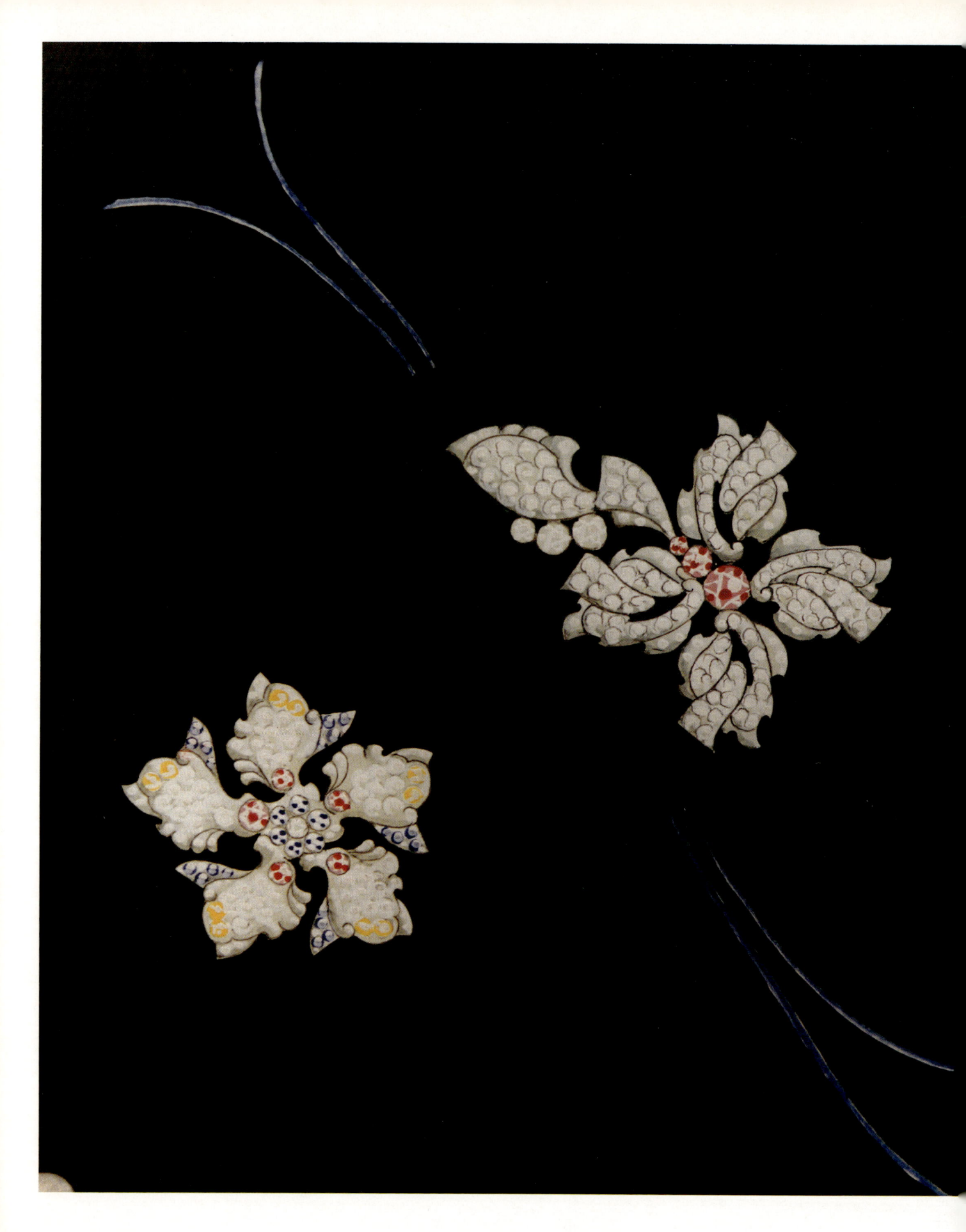

These tissue sketches from the 1940s were
brought to life in delicate watercolor renderings.

The Artist and the Craftsman

The designing of costume jewelry, which is most often viewed as the more glamorous side of the costume jewelry business, goes far beyond the mere act of transferring an innovative idea to paper. A broad knowledge of the manufacturing process is necessary in the transformation from initial design to reality. The concept must be viable from a manufacturing standpoint, or solvable if its unique qualities take it beyond the norm.

The designer must be not only an artist, but also well versed in every step of the process, so that financial considerations or labor-intensive procedures will be taken into account as the creation takes shape on the drawing board. This involves an understanding of not only what is occurring in the artist's own environment but also the conditions and restrictions in related industries. From top to bottom and beginning to end, everything must come under scrutiny, such as the findings and fasteners most suitable for the design, the quality and cost of the stones desired, and the time necessary from design concept to finished product. In other words, can the piece be "brought in" at a price that won't hamper the designer's artistic concept and still keep the manufacturer happy? Thus the creator is often forced to work within the frustrating barriers of manufacturing limitations...and that old bugaboo, cost! There's a fine line separating the artistic concept and finished product, and the designer must often tow it with more than a modicum of trepidation.

Following are two examples of the interplay between artist and craftsman that demonstrate how the seemingly diverse talents of each specialist merge, each one dependent upon the skills of the other.

Rendering

Jewelry rendering is the process of drawing the designer's concept so that it can be manufactured. Depending upon the complexity of the piece, this can evolve into an elaborate and time-consuming undertaking, requiring the presentation of each and every stone or pearl, for example, exactly as it will appear in the design. The rendering must also convey critical details, such as cuttings or designs in the metal base or any decorative embellishments, and it is this basic information that enables the initial manufacturing processes to begin. With the rendering process frequently requiring overlaying each individual step, one on top of the other, a more intricate piece can often involve a full week's work for one person.

Even so, a rendering is usually not a "working" drawing. It is instead an elaborate illustrated view, but not presented from the side or portraying actual depth. This is because the rendered drawing is initially used as a sales tool in presenting the design idea. If it is viable and the concept enthusiastically received, it can then advance to the "working" drawing stage. In some cases this becomes a multi-step process–one artist doing the rough sketch, another the actual rendering, and yet another the "working" drawing necessary for the model maker to proceed. Every minute detail, including all views and dimensions, must be completed before the initial steps of the manufacturing operation can begin.

The rendering techniques offer the artist an opportunity to bring his own particular expertise and preferences to the finished drawing. Some designers prefer to render in pencil, others in gold inks or with colored pencils. When applicable, still other designers favor the gouache technique, whereby overlapping layers of paint are built up on acetate, thus creating very effective overlays of color. Gouache rendering is an effective, beautiful, yet time-consuming process, one in which yet another highly skilled and artistic technique plays an elemental role in the creation of "costume jewelry masterpieces."

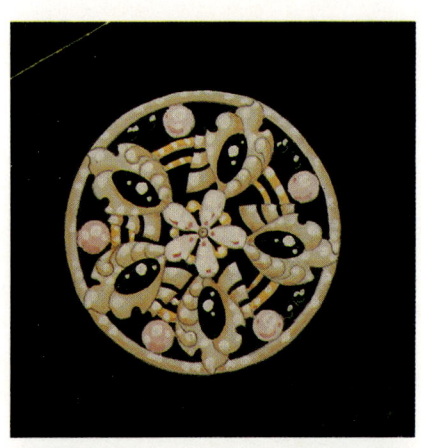

Model Making

The model maker's task is a tedious one. When the working drawing, or design, has been completed, which must include all specifications like height, width, measurements, contours, side walls, and textures, a sheet of properly-sized pewter stock is selected. A drawing of the design is glued to the stock and the basic shape cut out with a coping saw. In the case of three-dimensional designs, this might require cutting several different parts–such as figurals and flowers–to create the modeling effect needed. These parts would then be placed at various levels to create the required dimensions, with a soldering torch employed to fuse the pieces together again.

The actual modeling and shaping then begins, requiring the use of engraving tools, as well as skill in burring, the latter necessitating the operation of an electric, machine-driven mandrell with a foot pedal. Following shaping, the proper coarse and fine files are selected so that detailing on the face of the model can be completed. The piece must then be emoried, and further refined with steel wool.

At this stage, any excess metal has to be hollowed out of the back of the piece in order to keep the weight within workable limits. A spring gauge is used to measure all areas, making certain that it conforms to the 1.5mm necessary to ensure that there are no weak spots or blow holes in the eventual rubber mold. Depending on the style of the piece, pads are then placed for posts or clips (if earrings), or pin backs (if brooches), with the maker's logo, copyright, or patent material applied during this final stage.

Most often the result of many years in the apprentice system, modelmaking is a highly-demanding profession, with each artisan often developing individual preferences and skills. For example, some prefer to work exclusively with their own designs, while others hone specific areas of expertise, such as pavé work, and will only accept assignments requiring that particular skill.

When one fully considers the processes involved in making each piece of jewelry, we can but echo Graham Hughes' reflective observation:
"...it is a tricky road from craft to art...the craftsman gets paid by the hour...he is happy making other people's designs; he usually gets no personal credit...because somebody else's name...is imposed upon it...An artist, on the other hand, always wants his name affixed to his product, because every thing he makes is part of his personality...he usually dislikes repeating himself, so his livelihood is automatically insecure."[1]

The road Hughes so colorfully describes is indeed fraught with pitfalls, yet the utmost in personal satisfaction often lies around the bend. When all is said and done, however, the skills of the craftsman overlap those of the artist and vice versa, for the artist is also quite often the craftsman, and the craftsman the artist. One would be hard pressed to deny that many of the craftspeople so instrumental in fashioning the jewelry we admire today have earned the right to the title "artist"...and many an "artist" is most proud of the qualities that made him a craftsman. *Vivé la différence!*

The spirit of inventiveness and determination seems inbred in the species. To the credit of those who were not afraid to try and try again, centuries long past gave us times of heady experimentation and fearless triumphs. Those who were part of the jeweler's art were no exception in this scenario. In fact, "Up to Roman times, jewelers were intoxicated with their own skill...These craftsmen, like the societies in which they lived, felt they could do anything they tried."[2] *Jeweled masterpieces from the 20th century speak to us with much the same voice, for neither did the artisans who created them decades ago allow themselves to be bound by safe and more conventional techniques. They too were pioneers without fear of failure...driven by an unwavering determination to offer innovative designs that would appeal to people from all walks of life and all income categories.*

Presented here are several hundred prime examples of these costume jewelry "masterpieces" (of which there were, of course, countless thousands), concentrating most heavily on the 20th century, when costume jewelry as we know it today became an accepted adjunct to the female wardrobe. On the following pages are a cross-section of pieces that can still be uncovered by the average buyer and collector...that individual who appreciates beauty and fine workmanship in spite of the fact that they do not, for the most part, rely on precious metals and gems. Some are large and dynamic, others dainty and intricate. Some are astoundingly beautiful, still others merely whimsical, but with a charm that sets them apart. Whether chosen to wear or simply admire, each represents the diversified skills of one or many artisans, men and women whose devotion to their craft shines through as brightly as the glittering stones and brilliant enameling. Here is a legacy that cannot be denied them, for they built it piece by piece by piece!

1 Hughes, *The Art of Jewelry*, p. 242
2 Ibid., p. 14

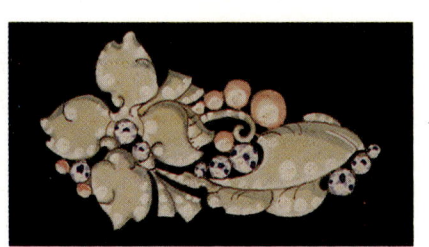

47

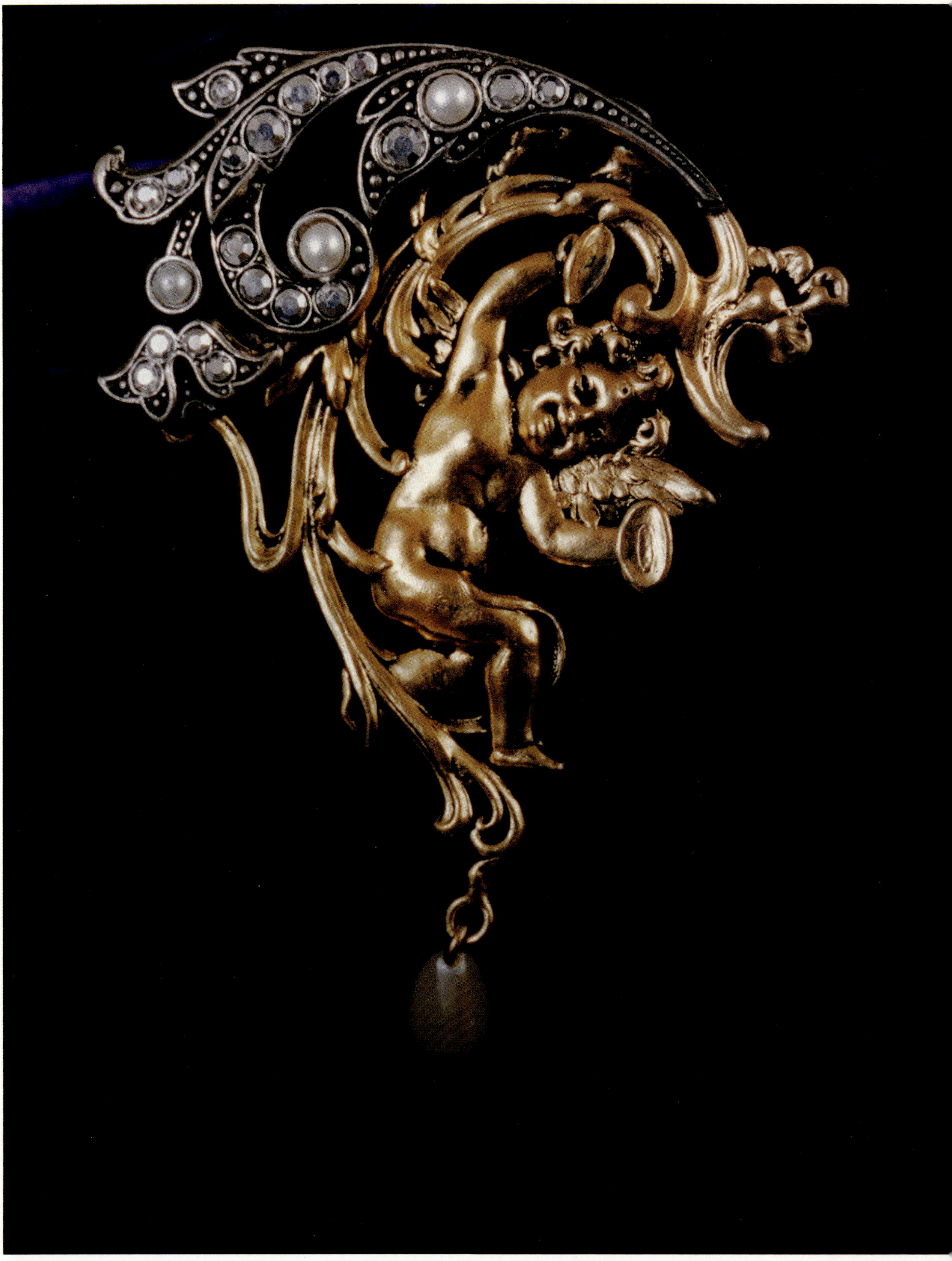

Marked and Memorable

During costume jewelry's heyday, hundreds of companies were involved in its design and manufacture. In some cases, a paper tag was attached to each piece, thus identifying the maker. In others, the name appeared on a plaque on the underside, or was stamped or engraved upon it. It is important to bear in mind, however, that many of the fine signed pieces we so admire today were wholly or partially the work of a host of jobbers. Among these were the large Circle Products organization, which manufactured pieces for many of the top operations in New York, but countless others were scattered throughout Rhode Island and New York City, serving as an invaluable link in the "jewelry chain."

Following are examples of masterpieces from some of the better known makers. They demonstrate a broad range of fine costume pieces from a wide variety of the best known designers and manufacturers of their day. Each is intended to represent the works of all those who contributed their energies and expertise during the mid-twentieth century, an exciting chapter in costume jewelry's history. By adhering to the credo that the quality of workmanship and design was paramount, they have earned a well-deserved place in the history of entrepreneurship.

With such an illustrious background, it becomes evident why these "jewels," some newly-plucked from long-forgotten jewelry cases, or even safe deposit boxes--have now become our treasured "friends."

From Accessocraft's 1969 "dragon" line. Designer, Milton Torem.

AMERICAN STYLE

From Accesocraft's Art Nouveau line of the late 1960s, both designed by Dorothy Torem.

Marked American Style Co., an unusual brooch with a cluster of off-center amethyst stones and fleur de lis accents. The design would indicate it is a piece from early in the century.

ACCESSOCRAFT

Accessocraft was founded by Edgar Rodelheimer and Theodore Steinman in the 1930s. Their offerings were unique in that they aptly combined both the "accessory" and "craft" elements of their name, thus expanding the entire jewelry category into a broader "accessories" range. This included fanciful buckles, opera glasses, and the magnifying glass pendants for which they are still renowned. The company is currently under the aegis of Theodore Steinman's son, Paul.

ART

Under the aegis of Arthur Pepper, the Art designation was extracted from the company name, ModeArt. Art pieces reflect a wide range of designs and varied techniques, and their unusual offerings generate "eye appeal" that attracts considerable attention in today's vintage jewelry market. The company was in operation from the 1940s until the 1970s.

Noted for their impressive and imaginative designs, a bracelet by Art.

McCLELLAND BARCLAY

Easily recognizable on sight and highly specialized in design, pieces marked McClelland Barclay reflect, most specifically, the beauty of Art Deco. In gold as well as silver finishes, an array of very specific designs formed the base for much of the jewelry bearing his name, their difference being solely in the outer shapes, the color of the stones, and their rhinestone overlay designs.

Barclay was renowned during the 1930s and early Forties for his magazine illustrations; however, his name can also be found on such varied items as sculpture, candlesticks, and bowls. His artistic talents were tragically and prematurely ended when he lost his life during World War II.

Not to be confused with "Barclay," another fine costume jewelry line that was manufactured during this period, McClelland Barclay pieces are distinctively marked with both names, although depending on its placement on the piece, part of the name might be obscured but nevertheless recognizable by the style of the remaining letters.

The strength of McClelland Barclay's deco designs shines through in this melange of brooches, accented by a pendant necklace and open-linked bracelet.

52

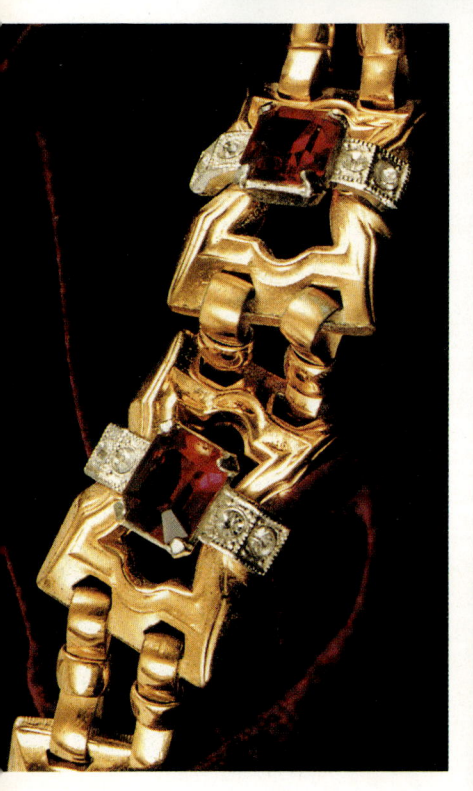

BIJOUX CASCIO

Bijoux Cascio was founded by Gaetano Cascio, and was a participant in the first showing of Italian Alta Moda in Florence in 1951, which served to undermine the stranglehold of French haute couture on international fashion. Bijoux Cascio was also renowned for accessorizing the creations of Emilio Pucci and Capucci, among others. By 1955, Bonwit Teller, Bloomingdale's, Lord & Taylor, and Henri Bendel were showcasing the Bijoux Cascio name for their fashionable clientele.

In 1970, Gaetano's son Ricardo succeeded his father, and by 1992 he had expanding the business from two boutique operations in Florence to fifty shops in and around Italy.

Bijoux Cascio jewelry is steeped in the family's heritage of Old World, guild-trained workmanship, the same traditional training that so many immigrants brought with them to America, and on which much of the U.S. costume jewelry industry was built.

Italian in origin and marked Bijoux Cascio, this 4" masterpiece is a testimonial to the legacy of Italian craftsmanship, which continued through succeeding generations and also left its mark on the American jewelry scene. Note how the tiny red stones are tightly embedded in mosaic-like fashion into the gold rimmed petals.

BOUCHER

The MB marking, which is difficult to read with its small rooster next to the letters, was used in the 1937-1938 timeframe; pieces also contain a style number in addition to the signature marking of either MB (for its founder, Marcel Boucher) or simply Boucher. Both Marcel Boucher and his wife Sandra began their careers in fine jewelry design, converting that skill to the production of upscale costume pieces fashioned with the same care as their "fine" counterparts.

In the late 1940s, Boucher introduced the three-dimension design in costume jewelry, an innovation that enabled him to convince a court, during his battle with the giant Coro empire, that his copyright of this design gave him exclusive rights.

Five years after Marcel Boucher's death in 1965, his wife and partner, Sandra Boucher, sold the business. She remains a force in the industry, teaching at the Fashion Institute of Technology in New York City and designing privately for other major jewelry operations.

Night and Day...from the glitter of rhinestones to the subtlety of gold and pearls, a Boucher brooch with ingenious pin back slide that enables it to be reversible at the wearer's whim.

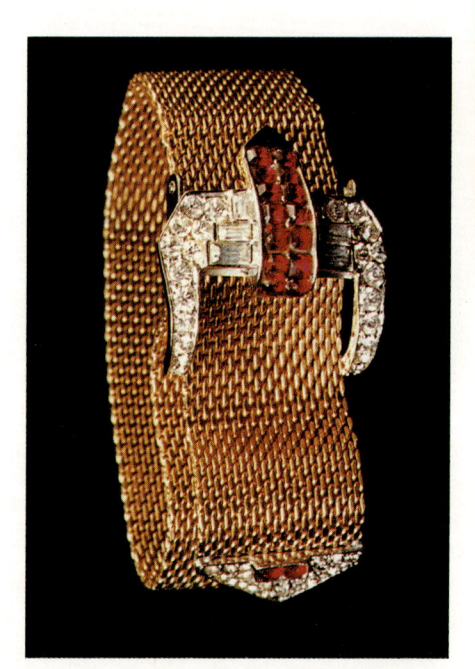

In a gold mesh design, a Boucher cuff with "buckle" accents.

54

And Day and Night! Again by Boucher, this one even features an enameled beetle on the gold leaf "day time" side.

The look for which Boucher is noted. In the "fine" jewelry tradition, a pearl-centered brooch and earrings set.

55

BRANIA

CADORO

Founded after World War II, and executed with impeccable skill, Cadoro reflected the bold artistic acumen and strong influence of the worldwide travels of its partners, Dan Steneskieu and actor Steve Brody. The business continued for only a few years after Steneskieu's death in the mid-1970s. Cadoro pieces are among the finest to be found today, each bearing the imprint of these ingenious gentlemen, who were determined to imbue their jewelry with imaginative designs and a "touch of class." They succeeded most admirably.

Close-up of huge, elaborate clasp on a black beaded necklace with pink, green and clear stones and crystal rondels, signed Brania. Brania was an exclusive New York bead house, with Mimi d 'N responsible for many of their designs during a short period in the early 1960s.

BURKS

What a charmer! With its nacreous pearlized "body" and jade eye, this mythological fish by Cadoro has a mystical quality that speaks volumes.

Studded with faux lapis and emerald cabochons, this whimsical frog by Cadoro is plump and happy!

By Burks of Canada, this brooch, sparkling like diamonds and sapphires, has all the beauty of its fine jewelry counterparts and, in addition to the regular clasp, includes an unusual chain/clip arrangement for added security.

Massive in weight and carefully crafted, this Cadoro bracelet differs greatly from many costume jewelry bracelets that simply have "push-in" clasps. The rhinestone "H" bar that covers it is moveable and hinged, giving the bracelet a smooth and upscale look like that found in fine jewelry. There are also seven interlocking links, each connected by two separate, overlapping links of rhinestones.

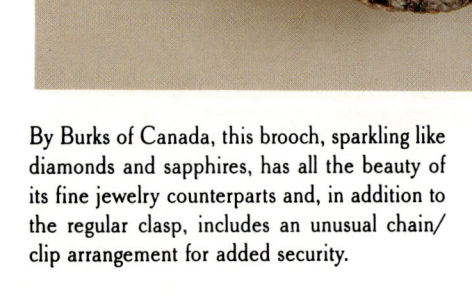

This Cadoro cuff is of two paws, each centered with faux lapis stones.

CALVAIRE

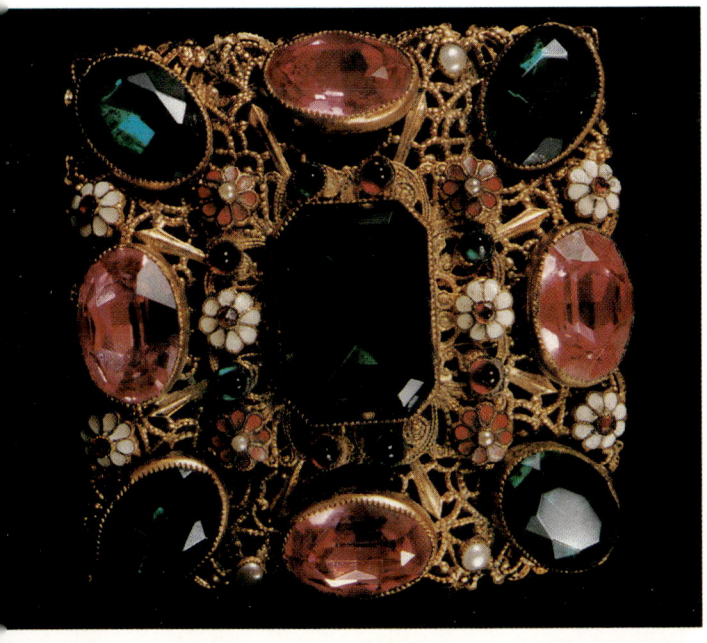

HATTIE CARNEGIE

Viennese born (as Hattie Kanengeiser), Hattie Carnegie's family emigrated to the United States when she was six years old. Her background in fashion included both millinery and couture, later expanding into jewelry and fragrance. One of her early jewelry designers was Norman Norell, who joined

Skillfully enameled, this 2.5" brooch and earrings parure by Hattie Carnegie has textured leaves with delicate ridges, every carefully-constructed detail making a somewhat "commonplace" subject masterfully crafted in a most "uncommon" way.

Although featured on the cover of *Costume Jewelers, The Golden Age of Design*, this brooch is worthy of a closer look. Signed Calvaire and with a decidedly European flavor, here is a swedged design with enameling, pearls, tiny cabochons, and giant foil-backed stones, all on an amazingly intricate casting–a piece that must have taken an enormous number of hours to complete.

Carnegie in 1920 and later established himself independently in the couture field, as did Pauline Trigere, who also worked for Carnegie in the 1930s. Another fine jewelry designer, Peggy Moonan, provided free-lance designs for Carnegie, so too did the wonderful sportswear designer Claire McCardell, who joined the Carnegie organization in 1939. Interestingly, McCardell established her own jewelry company, Van S. Authentics, in the late 1950s-early Sixties. Nadine Effront, a student of Georges Braque, designed many unusual Carnegie pieces with a foreign flavor, in keeping with Carnegie's interest in jewelry featuring figurals and Eastern, Oriental, and Greek themes. At the other end of the Carnegie jewelry spectrum were sparkling beads and intricate designs with unusual combinations of stones. Instrumental in many of Carnegie's later designs was her nephew, Irving Apisdorf, who also served as vice president of the organization.

Several years after Carnegie's death in 1956, the rights to her jewelry business were sold to Larry Josephs–who had formerly spent nine years with Robert Originals. Production of the Carnegie line ceased in the 1970s.

A regal 2.25" swan by Hattie Carnegie is testimony to the effectiveness of tastefully intermingled materials. Here are carved composition ivory feathers and a composition head and neck, accented with gold marbleized enameling, tiny rhinestones, and glittering faux emeralds.

A lithe beauty by Hattie Carnegie, enameled in an effective, combination of rust/orange tones, accented with white.

In a glistening gold setting, the detail on this Hattie Carnegie necklace is astounding...soft green glass flowers, flecked with gold, are accented by dainty gold wires, each capped with a tiny crystal.

Shivering pansies! This trembler set by Hattie Carnegie has a textured antiqued finish accented with pearls, faux turquoise, amethysts, and "diamonds."

Hattie Carnegie zebra and purple marmot, both enameled and bejeweled.

This Hattie Carnegie burro carries a "valuable" back pack of pink and blue beads and matching crystals.

59

CASTLECLIFF

Founded by Clifford Furst in the 1940s, Castlecliff jewelry reflects the strong influence of that exciting period in costume jewelry's history. Their chief designer was William Markle, whose architectural background resulted in highly-stylized designs, making Castlecliff jewelry particularly attractive to collectors and all those who appreciate beauty and precision in fine costume jewelry. The company ceased operations in the 1960s.

Both from the same design period, this is Castlecliff at its finest. The domed prong-set brooch is centered with an enormous faceted crystal; the bracelet of matching shades of iridescent blue-green has lustrous, diamond-shaped foiled stones.

Dynamic but delicate, a vermeil brooch by Castlecliff has sparkling miniature rhinestones accented with a plethora of tiny dangling pearls.

Castlecliff pendant on heavy gold chain; multi-hued enamel with turquoise colored stone. Note the four "kissing Indians" couples.

Intertwining gold tendrils curl seductively around a pave center with tremblers. This brooch and earrings parure is by Castlecliff.

Sunny days from Castlecliff...yellow stones of varied hues, with a marbleized composition clasp and matching brooch.

New stocking choice: brown

Four stockings that follow (beautifully) the fashion for brown, and lead in a fascinating new direction: namely, toward a special new kind of stocking darkness. It's semi-darkness, really: this subtle shading of brown that thins to almost nothing on the leg, leaving a delicate trace of veiling, moulding, tinting.

At left: Dark and delicate and meant for black-brown mixtures, polished brown fabrics: the shade Belle-Sharmeer calls "Diamond Mink."

At right: On the dark taupe side: delicious with same: "Brilliant Brown" by Hummingbird. Good with soft, deep browns; black, too.

At left: To wear with winebrown, plumbrown, and with red (when the shoe is brown): "Paris Brown" stockings by Christian Dior.

At right: The golden one among the browns: Mary Grey's "Jazz," wonderful with amber, camel's hair, any golden brown. Announcement of the return Everywhere here: Announcement of the return of a bracelet that's almost a fashion legend—the three-strand, diamond-clasped bracelet of the twenties, here in copies that would fool a second-storey man. These, and all other bracelets here, by Castlecliff, at Altman's; Hutzler's; Harzfeld's; I. Magnin,

The triple-strand bracelet of blue glass beads and interlocking rhinestone clasp is by Castlecliff. Its pearl companion with a Deco-style rhinestone center is marked Panetta. The Belle-Sharmeer stocking ad from the mid-1950s, featuring the same Castlecliff bracelet, reads:
"Announcement of the return of a bracelet that's almost a fashion legend—the three-strand diamond-clasped bracelet of the twenties, here in copies that would fool a second-storey man. These, and all other bracelets here, by Castlecliff."

A magnificent Castlecliff brooch with domed layers encircling a clear center stone.

ALICE CAVINESS

Alice Caviness founded the company bearing her name in 1945. She was later joined by a partner, Lois Stevens. Caviness died in 1983, but Stevens continues as the designer today. As in the past, Caviness pieces are only available in the specialty shop venue.

An Alice Caviness masterpiece in this bracelet/earrings combination featuring all manner of chunky and confetti stones accented by multi-shaped, offset crystals. The close-up gives added impetus to a powerful design.

Bouquet de fleur mélanges fait un clip en émail multicolore et or. –Chanel brooch from an illustration by E. Lindner in the April 1938 issue of *Vogue*.

CHANEL

The Chanel name epitomizes "individuality." Born Gabrielle, she will always be remembered as "Coco." A trendsetter in couture fashions, her empire flourished during the teen years of this century and the "roaring Twenties." By 1938 she had 4,000 people in her employ worldwide. With the onset of World War II in 1939, her couture operation was halted, remaining in limbo throughout the remainder of the war years. However, largely due to a scandal regarding her personal involvement with a member of the German military, she wisely decided to wait until 1954 before resuming her businesses.

Like Elsa Schiaparelli, Chanel was a pioneer in bringing widespread acceptance of costume jewelry to the public and quick to recognize the impact of bold accessories on high-style, understated garments. Count Etienne de Beaumont was one of her designers, as was Fulco Santo Stefano della Cerda, Duke of Verdura, who was responsible for one of Chanel's most popular jewelry items, the rigid bracelet featuring black and white enamel centered with a dramatic multi-stone Maltese cross. This particular design was inspired by a similar fine jewelry bracelet that was given to Coco by Grand Duke Dmitri of Russia. Early Chanel jewelry also bears the influence of Maison Gripoix of Paris, who started with her in 1924 and is responsible for the now-famous *"Fleurs e'maileés,"* ("enamel flowers"); these were, however, not enameled at all, but instead featured glass paste flowers executed in a wide range of colors. One of Chanel's later designers was the noted Robert Goosens, who worked from his own shop in the mid-1950s and created many of her important jewelry designs.

Vintage Chanel jewelry is highly-sought in today's collecting marketplace...and Chanel jewelry of more recent vintage is just as treasured, not only for its beauty and wearability now, but also for its collectible value in years to come.

From the 1940s, this regal necklace by Chanel looks like it could decorate the portrait of a French courtesan at Versailles! The intricate design gives clear evidence that the look of fine jewelry was masterfully duplicated in well-executed "French paste" and faux pearls.

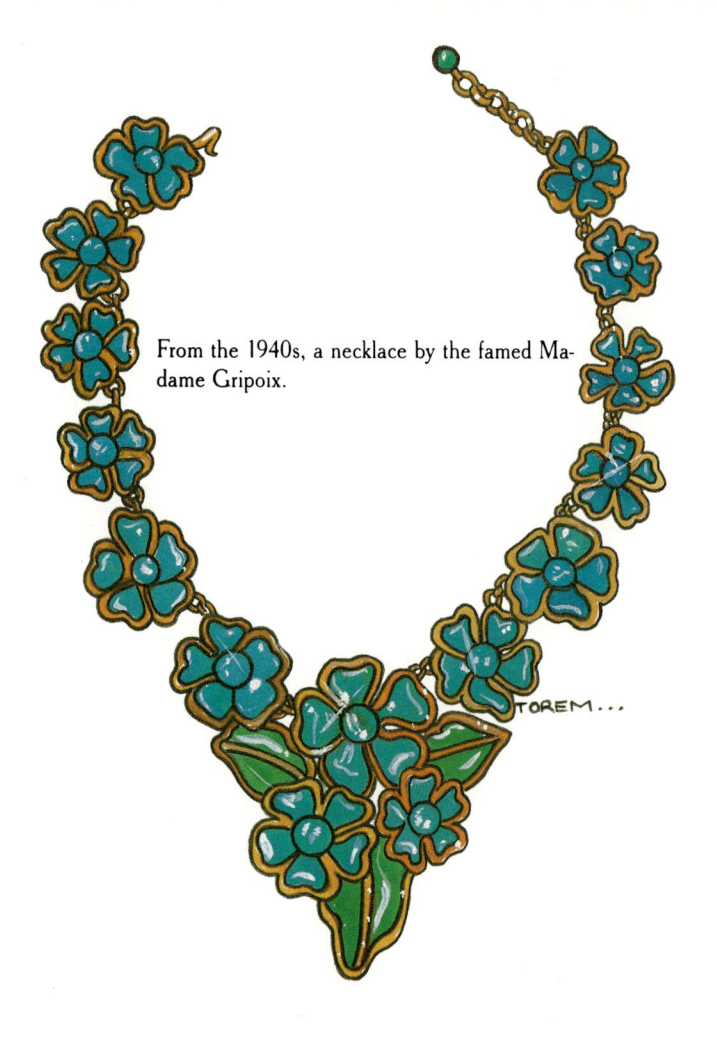

From the 1940s, a necklace by the famed Madame Gripoix.

A riot of pearls and red stones, this three-strand mabe pearl necklace is by Chanel.

A melange of twenty-five years of Chanel.

64

Chanel...Chanel...Chanel–in a splendid mix of vintage and new. Here is a vintage necklace by Gripoux, a script-signed vintage brooch, and a Maltese cross from the 1990s.

An early piece in an exciting Chanel design, this stylized flamingo is script-signed and features rose-cut, pre-set stones.

Curling seductively, a colorful enamel and rhinestone brooch by Chanel, script signed.

Dangling succulently from the ears...blown glass grapes with gold-veined, enameled leaves. By Chanel.

Script-signed Chanel brooch from the 1930s or early '40s; the fruit is glass with enamel.

A long belt/necklace by Chanel. Dated 1982, each link is detachable, making it possible to change designs and lengths. Note crackled amethyst stones, indicative of Gripoux.

Cheery cherries! Contemporary Chanel earrings of muted resin and crackled stones.

From the 1980s, a giant cuff bracelet and celestial globes for the ears that remind one of orbiting bodies in a black, black sky. By Chanel.

Leaping dolphins...from the 1980s, unbelievable acrylic cuff bracelets. Note the Chanel logo in the eyes.

This luminous gardenia rises in gold-rimmed layers accented with enamel leaves. By Chanel, and of current design, it is reminiscent of a 1940's Debutante Cotillion. Adding to the nostalgic ambiance is the gold sequinned Chanel flower in the background.

Ancient coins...Chanel recreates them in a massive bracelet of current genre.

68

At home in the deep...Chanel coral starfish earrings, accented by logo-topped pearls.

Close-up of a contemporary, heavily-chained rope featuring pearls and unusual beads. By Chanel.

These delightful Ciner angels carry the "scatter pin" to heavenly heights!

In keeping with Ciner's expertise with beautiful beaded ropes of fine quality stones, these long strands of clear lucite have rhinestone spacers; the "horse and bit" clasp can be worn to the side.

With heavy square links in a brushed florentine finish accented with rhinestones, this Ciner bracelet reflects an Art Deco influence.

CINER

Founded by Emanuel Ciner in 1892, Ciner has the distinction of being the only company that converted from the production of fine jewelry to costume pieces exclusively. During the Depression era, their faux diamonds were synthetic white sapphires imported from France, and this practice of never stinting on the quality and uniqueness of their stones and beads has continued ever since.

Ciner was also responsible for g[iv]ing impetus to the use of wax molds (li[ke] those used by dentists) instead of t[he] previously popular sand casting metho[d]. Their designs are copper-plated fir[st] then nickel-plated, after which they a[re] electroplated in gold. Still creating ma[s]terpieces that reflect the influence [of] their founder, Ciner's current offerin[gs] with special emphasis on their ropes a[nd] multiple-strand necklaces, are t[he] epitome of beauty and quality, and mu[ch] in demand today.

CORO

Coro, founded in the late Twenties, was at one time the largest manufacturer of costume jewelry in the world–selling a stupendous $33 million per year at their peak, a figure that would be equivalent to considerably more by today's dollar value. The Coro name combined the first two letters of the last names of its founders, Cohn and Rosenberger. Although the inroads made by couture designers played a major role in establishing costume jewelry as a more acceptable accessory item, Coro was at the forefront of bringing it to the mass market. This resulted in high-end pieces like the sterling ones found in their upscale CoroCraft line and the high end of Coro, as well as very inexpensive, but charming, Coro baubles that could be plucked from the counter of five and dimes across the country.

Through much of Coro's long history, Adolph Katz was responsible for Coro's team of designers and for their marketing choices. His merchandising genius enabled the company to meet the wide-ranging needs of the exploding costume jewelry venue. Among his top designers was Selwyn Young, who contributed many of the outstanding 1940's designs, later joining the Lisner jewelry organization. Another was Anthony Aquilino, who later formed his own company, Anthony Creations. Also contributing to early Coro designs were the Verrecchia brothers, Gene and Reno, who later founded GemCraft, a company that still remains in operation in Providence, Rhode Island.

In addition to CoroCraft, *Vendome* (which succeeded CoroCraft) and *Francoise* (a short-lived but beautiful line) were also branches of the Coro conglomerate. In the 1970s, the old Coro enterprises ceased their operations.

A dynamic CoroCraft sterling chatelaine with overtones of the military. The advertisement is from 1951.

This Mongolian warrior astride an Arabian steed is by CoroCraft.

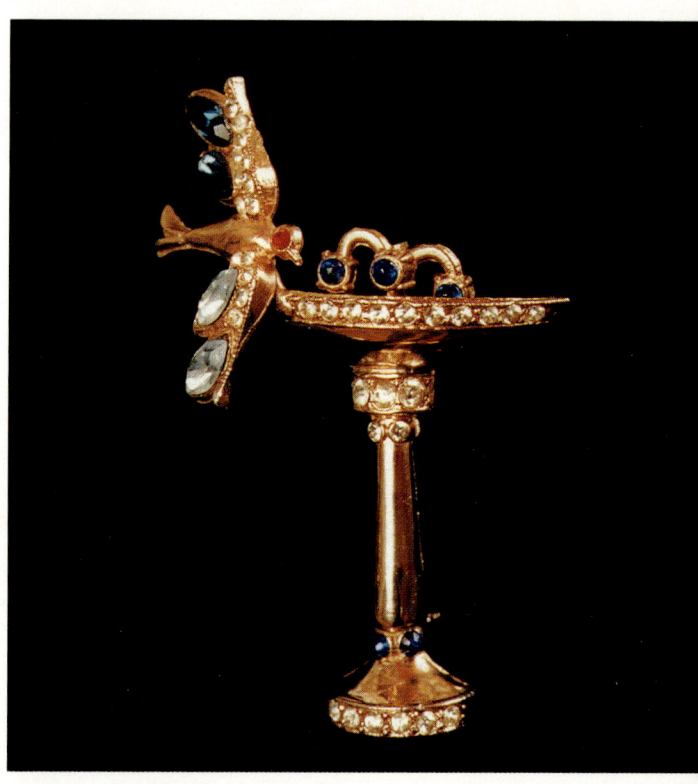

The whimsy for which Coro was famous...here, a jeweled birdbath brooch with glittery bird "perched for a drink."

Enamel flowers amid the enamel flowers! At the top is a large unsigned piece; in the center a pink sterling CoroCraft fur clip.

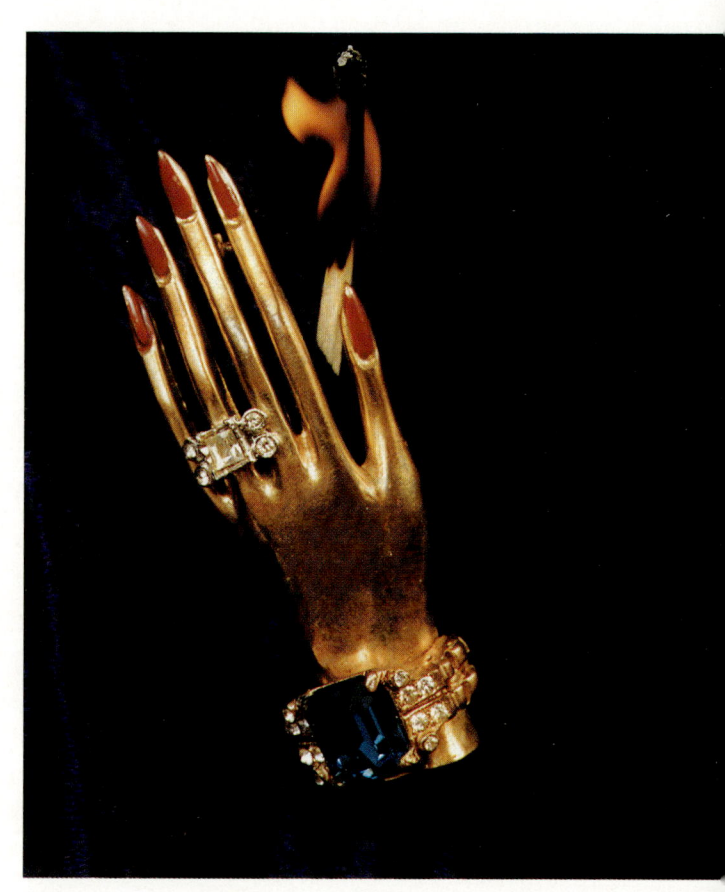

The glamour of the Forties...CoroCraft sterling brooch with enameled, manicured nails, showy "diamond" ring, and "sapphire"-centered bracelet.

By CoroCraft, this design departs from the "standard" crown look circa the 1930s and Forties that remains so popular today. This one is particularly charming with its aquamarine stones encased in individual gold-lined compartments.

Topsy turvy and fashioned after the finest of "fine" jewelry, Coro deserves credit for this glittering duo, circa 1940.

Early Coro. Heavily goldplated, enameled flower brooch with tiny blue stones peeking from its opened bud.

For the birds...Coro offered several duette designs in the ever-popular dual birds motif. This duo of black diamonds and enameling is seen less frequently than most of its feathered companions.

Lovebirds...a charming enameled Coro Duette in luscious shades of rose.

Bumblin' along...2.75" sterling Coro Duette, gold and pave stones with champleve accents.

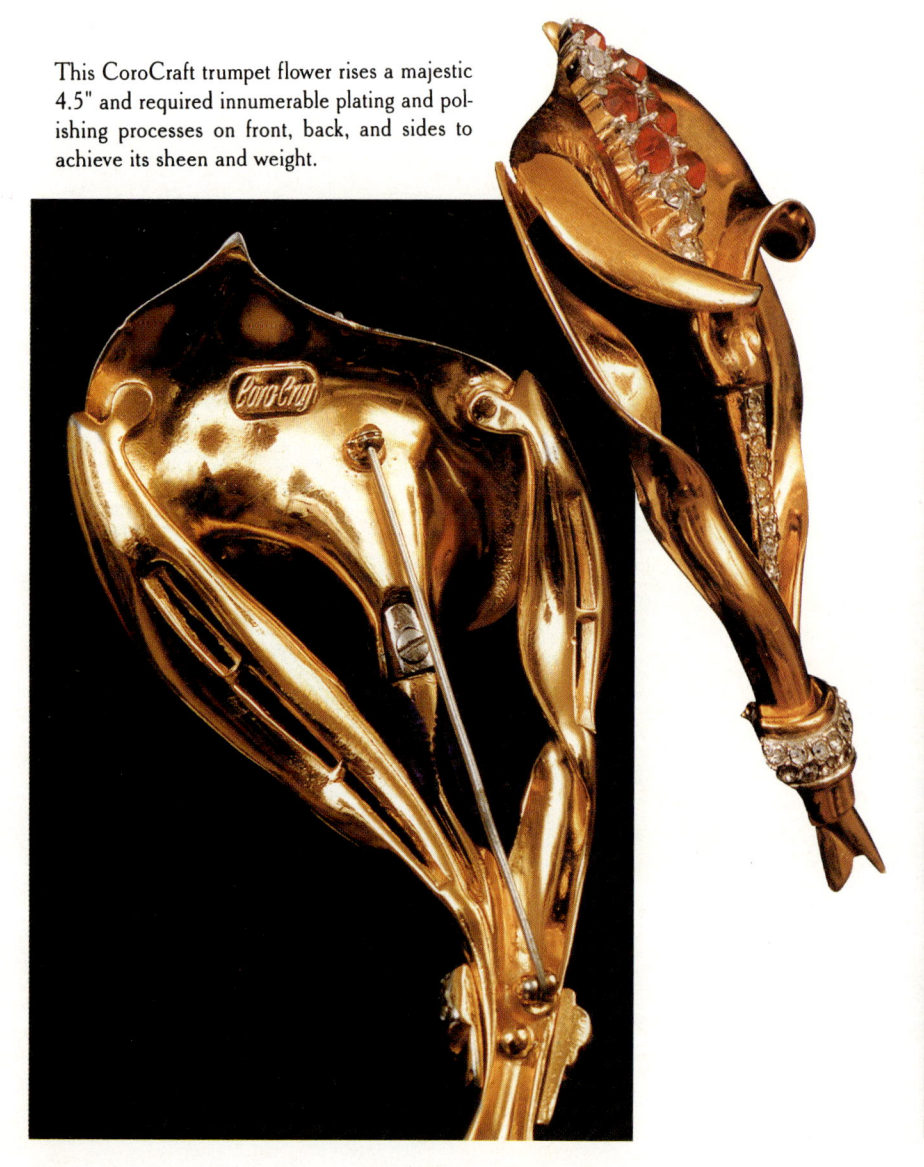

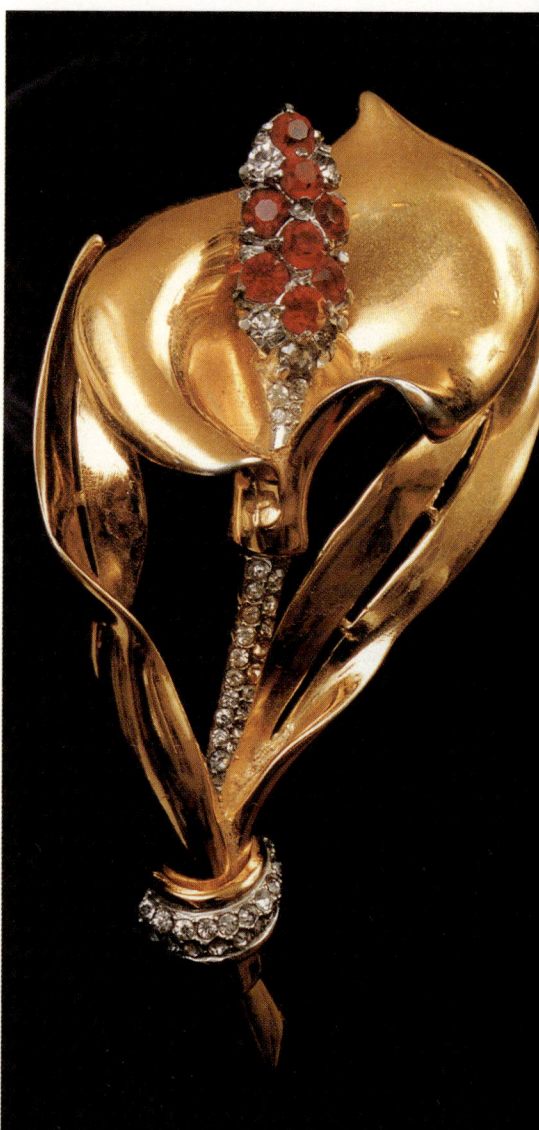

This CoroCraft trumpet flower rises a majestic 4.5" and required innumerable plating and polishing processes on front, back, and sides to achieve its sheen and weight.

74

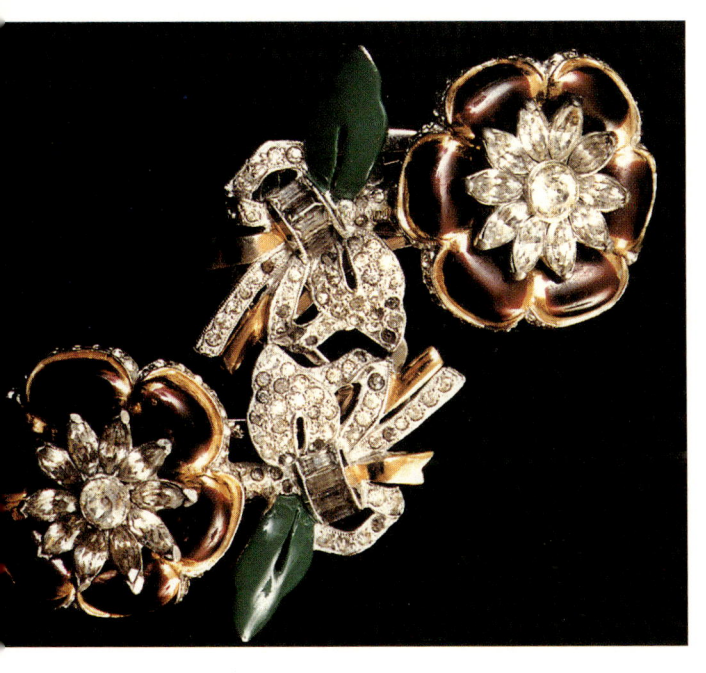

Two rarely seen Coro Duettes, both featuring an array of stones accented with enameling.

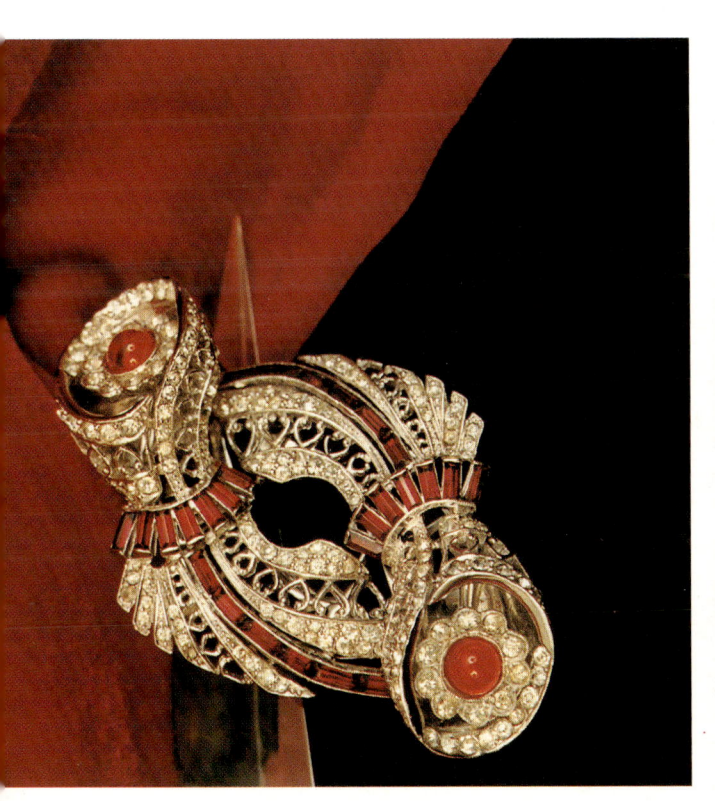

"Rubies and diamonds"...a 3" Coro Duette with classic lines and exquisite detail.

Signed Coro, a sterling (vermeil) brooch in the Art Nouveau genre. With its intricate "veining," this is a fine example of the artistry required for such delicate enameling.

75

VENDOME

Part of the Coro empire, Vendome was established in the 1950s as successor to the high-end CoroCraft line, with illustrious results. Although Coro's Adolph Katz oversaw some of the designs, Helen Marion served as their chief designer and guiding force. Especially renowned for beautiful strands of beads and crystals, their other offerings were also noteworthy for their complex designs and innovative use of stones.

The unusual design of this Vendome brooch is further accentuated by not only the shapes of the stones but also their deep-hued, regal colors.

A magnificent combination of colors, materials and design makes this 3.5" brooch by Vendome both beautiful and delightful. Acrylic clear petals with center sections of red and clear rhinestones rest on a japanned stalk with a single leaf veined with red rhinestones. The flowers are moveable.

Golden tusked elephant in marbleized taupe finish by Vendome.

A wonderful manipulated bead-on-wire Vendome brooch measuring 1.5" x 1.75". Opaque yellow and white beads, crystal rondels, and cut crystal stones complete the free-form flower. Just the piece to accent a pink, yellow and cream suit (a la Chanel) in the early Sixties–a look revived in mid-'90s fashions.

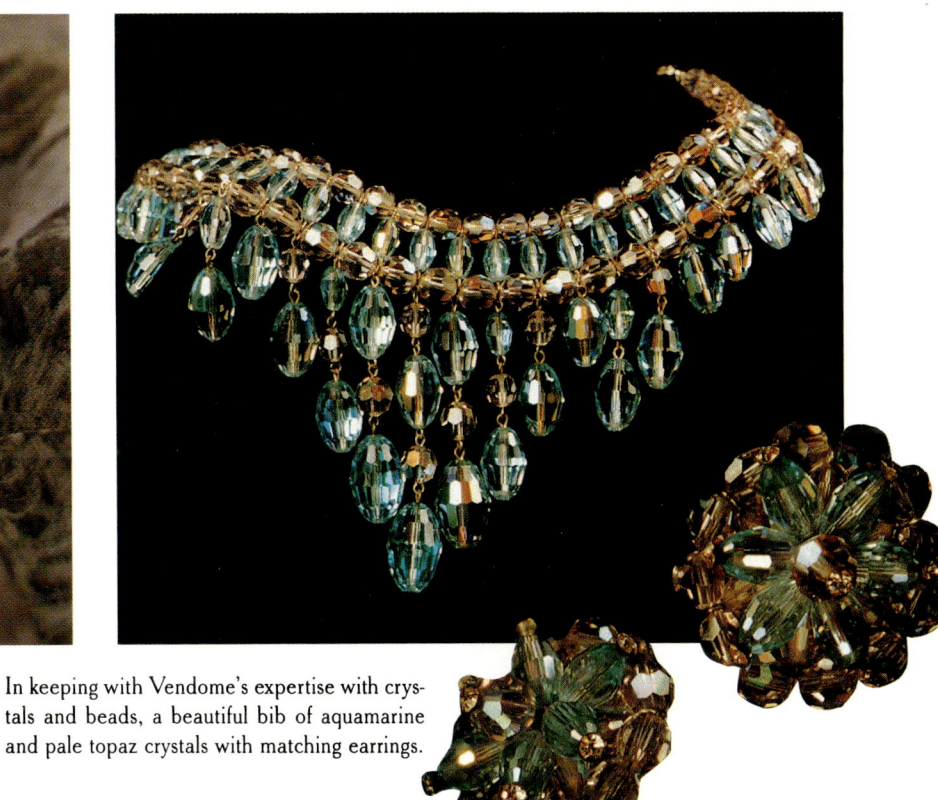

In keeping with Vendome's expertise with crystals and beads, a beautiful bib of aquamarine and pale topaz crystals with matching earrings.

FRANCOISE

Dangling its pearls and crystals, a lush Vendome wrap bracelet.

Signed Francoise, this 2.5" x 1.75" brooch is finely paved in crystals, faux topaz, and "black diamonds."

77

DeLILLO

DeLillo jewelry was founded by William DeLillo and Robert Clark (Clark was formerly a designer for Miriam Haskell and also one of her vice presidents). A native of Belgium, DeLillo came to the U.S. in the early 1950s, working for both Cartier and Harry Winston. A native of Pittsburgh, Pennsylvania, Clark replaced Frank Hess as head designer at Miriam Haskell in 1957, but left in 1967 to begin his business venture with DeLillo. They were later responsible for designing many pieces for the haute couture collections of both Nina Ricci and Schiaparelli.

Considered art jewelry, DeLillo pieces were created more exclusively than most, with their unusual "sculpture jewelry" extending into the 1980s and special designs created on a private-client basis.

Flecked with gold, a long DeLillo rope of polished lapis lazuli stones in an elaborate melange of shapes and sizes.

DeMARIO

Erroneously confused with Robert and its founder Robert Levy, the DeMario jewelry line was founded by Robert DeMario in the mid-1940s, a venture that came to an end some fifteen years later. Those years produced exquisite pieces, many with similar beading, hand wiring, and pearl details as those pioneered by Miriam Haskell. One of DeMario's designers was Mimi di N, who joined him for a short period in 1959.

DeROSA

The New York-based Ralph DeRosa Company had offices at 404 Fourth Avenue. DeRosa jewelry was produced from 1935 to 1955, a period during which many prime examples of the very finest costume jewelry is to be found. DeRosa is considered among the highest echelon of this group. A family operation, others prominently involved included Elvira, Virginia, and Theresa DeRosa.

Masters of enameling, this DeRosa flower has an almost primitive elegance.

By DeMario...an ornate bracelet of pearls and topaz beads, with matching earrings.

Her majesty...the Queen! This regal 3.5" DeRosa swan brooch has everything–giant clear amber stones, a magnificent blue center, heavy gold plating, and a grace and style that sets it apart from the ordinary.

DiNICOLA

Founded by Jerry DiNicola in the late 1950s-early Sixties period, the company became an arm of the large Capri jewelry operation in the mid-Sixties, but the DiNicola name no longer appeared after the early Seventies.

Quality casting was one of the hallmarks of DiNicola; these two brooches attest to their expertise in both design and execution.

This high-domed brooch by DiNicola has purity of design, and the ever-present quality of its casting.

80

MIMI di N

A descendant of Sicilian nobility and a member of the celebrated Fulco di Verdura family, Mimi di Niscemi was raised in both Sicily and Philadelphia. She is married to the grandnephew of Czar Nicolas II, Prince Alexander Romanoff.

Known as Mimi di N in the jewelry world, and with a background in both silversmithing and goldsmithing, she worked in partnership with Arnold Scaasi during the 1950s. In 1959 she joined DeMario, and later moved to Brania, a renowned New York bead house that also produced many fine pieces under the Brania name.

Mimi di N founded her own business in New York City in 1962, where she began working with manipulated pieces, a skill she had honed earlier with the Schiaparelli operation. She applies her abilities much as a sculptress would, first fashioning the pieces in clay. Combined with her silversmithing and goldsmithing talents, the quality of the results is unquestionable, for Mimi di N pieces are always a feast for the eyes and a delight to those who appreciate complex designs that are negotiated with the utmost skill.

After 1970, the original block-lettered logo bearing the Mimi di N name was replaced by a square tag stamped into the logo, along with the date.

In 3" layers that rise in Medieval splendor, the exhilarating height of this Mimi d'N piece was accomplished by swedging two well-modeled pieces together. For this particular design, swedging involved connecting the individual layers with pins, one side fitting into rivets on the opposite. Because of the limited mold sizes available at the time, achieving this height would have been impossible without using the swedging process. Additionally, as work progressed, its weight would have caused increasing difficulties for those entrusted with the finishing details. Before swedging this particular design, both pieces were plated with silver, and then "stop off" (a paint that can later be removed with acetone) was applied around the areas where the crystals would later be set. Each section was then goldplated, after which the "stop-off" was removed, leaving only those tiny portions rimming the crystals still in silver. Though obviously time-consuming and labor intensive, this added an effective but understated beauty to the finished piece. In addition to the large center stones, featured here are 120 1.5 and 2.0 millimeter, no-hole, turquoise beads, as well as over 70 handset, paved Swarovski crystals. This is an outstanding example of costume jewelry that equals the design and craftsmanship to be found in the best of "fine" jewelry. (The side-view photograph gives a detailed view of the layering, swedging process.)

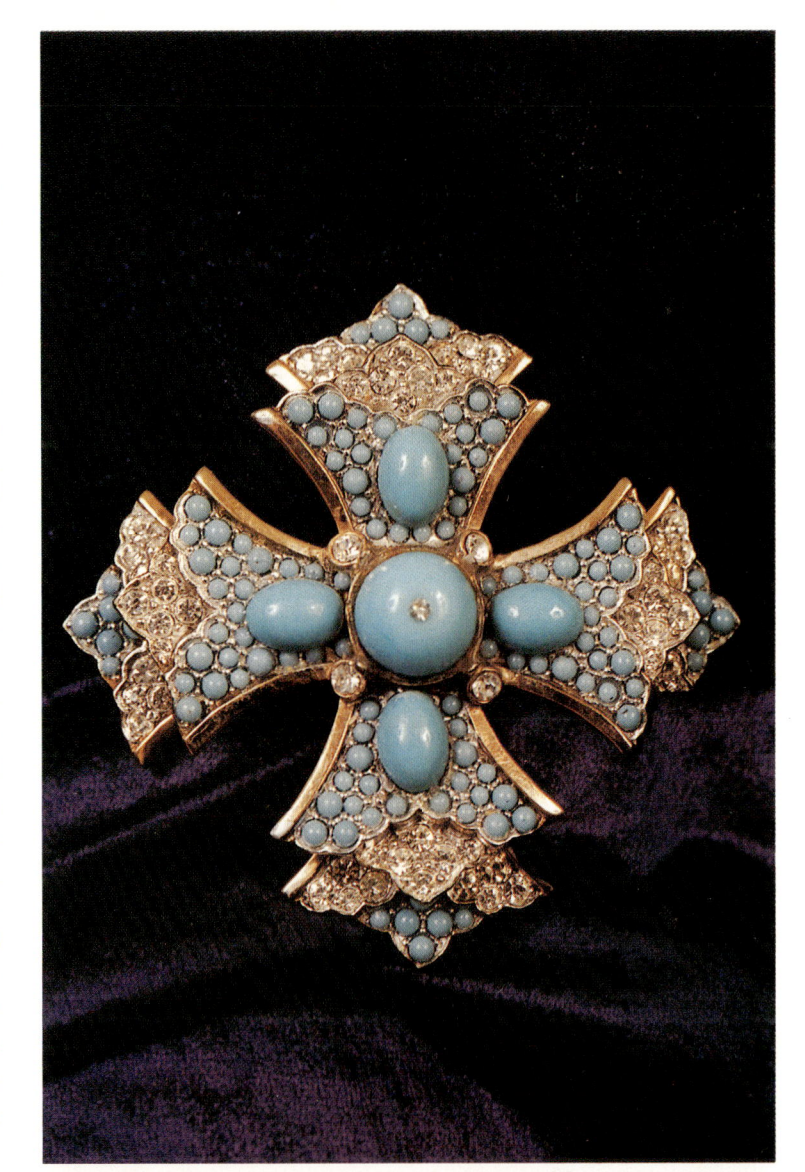

81

Mimi d'N created this necklace of woven beads, filigree balls, and tiny spacers.

Mimi d'N brooch with cabochons encased in gold "nests."

Mimi d'N does it again...giant turquoise stones are featured in another "striking" layered design. 2.75", this one is reminiscent of the lightning bolts of Thor!

EISENBERG

The Eisenberg saga has become legend in the costume jewelry industry. Founded by Jonas Eisenberg, an Austrian immigrant, they were originally a Chicago-based dress manufacturing business, flourishing during the early decades of this century. However, the novel addition of clips and brooches as an added bonus on many of their dresses inadvertently caused them to "turn the corner" from garments to glitter! (It's interesting to note that Oreste Agnini, founder of ORA jewelry, which was also based in Chicago, supplied the early brooches and clips that were an adjunct to Eisenberg's dresses.)

Perhaps not surprisingly, the idea of jewelry as part of the frock prompted mass shoplifting of these baubles, leading the Eisenbergs to conclude that "costume" jewelry might offer an even greater retailing opportunity than the garment trade. The rest is history, and Eisenberg is credited with being responsible for something most American women have taken for granted for decades—separate departments devoted exclusively to the sale of costume jewelry, and from that time on a mainstay in large emporiums throughout the country.

During the 1940 to 1972 period, Ruth M. Kamke was one of Eisenberg's chief designers.

Continuing a tradition that has evolved through three generations, Eisenberg jewelry now rests in the hands of Jonas' grandson, Karl. Currently called Eisenberg Classics (and so marked as either Eisenberg Classics or Eisenberg Ice) all pieces are readily identifiable by the date that follows the marking. These current pieces are made of platinum over sterling silver and the prongs are hand-polished (a step that wasn't taken in their early jewelry). The dentelles (32-facet stones) are available only in Europe and supplied exclusively to them by Swarovski of Austria. All Eisenberg Classics pieces are produced in the United States, enabling the company to maintain tight control over production methods, thereby ensuring the level of quality on which Eisenberg has built its impeccable reputation. They are among today's most illustrious "masterpieces."

The glory of Eisenberg.

"E" for Eisenberg–and enormous...a multi-faceted stone looks ripe for the plucking in this Eisenberg Original fur clip.

84

85

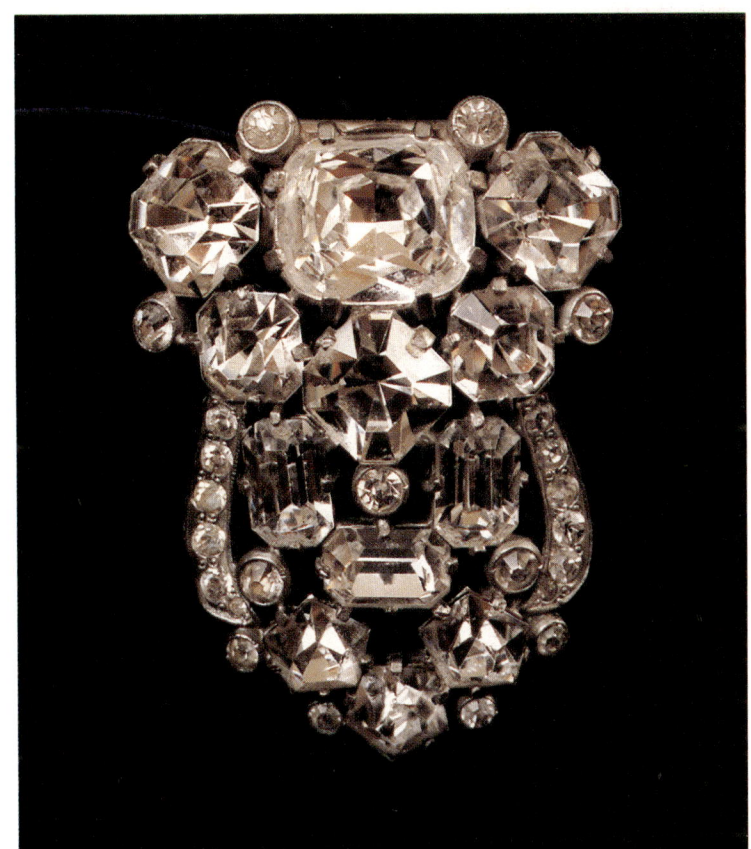

All marked either Eisenberg (in early scrolled marking) or Eisenberg Original, these designs and those on previous pages, mostly in sterling, are from the 1930s or early Forties.

With silver backing, this Eisenberg parure (with close-up of the bracelet's center section) features a sophisticated faux emerald/diamond combination and is from the 1950s.

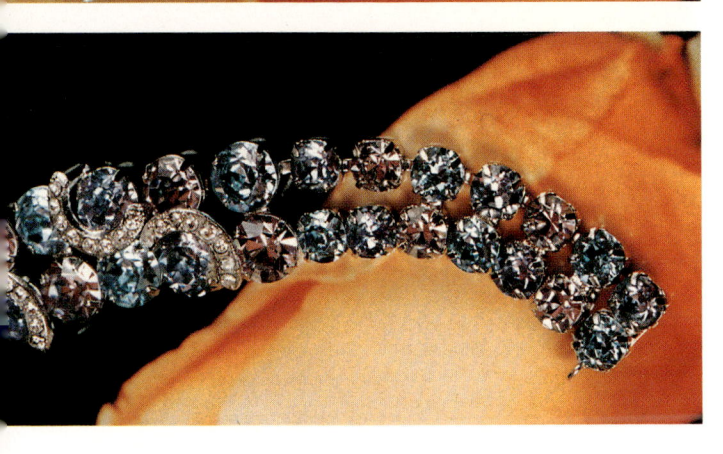

This Eisenberg parure, in a melding of shades of blue with pale lavender, gives testimony to the striking color combinations often found in Eisenberg designs. This set dates from the 1950s.

87

With giant amethyst stones, a stunning brooch by Eisenberg, circa 1950s.

The mysteries of Egypt in a heavily-plated pendant, glowing with vivid enameling. This was a dramatic departure from the classic pieces for which Eisenberg is noted, and part of a 1970s line inspired by the Tutankhamen exhibits.

The new Eisenberg Classics...every bit as exquisite as their earlier counterparts. Pieces courtesy of Karl Eisenberg. Photos by Dorothy Torem; model, Michele Courtois.

88

89

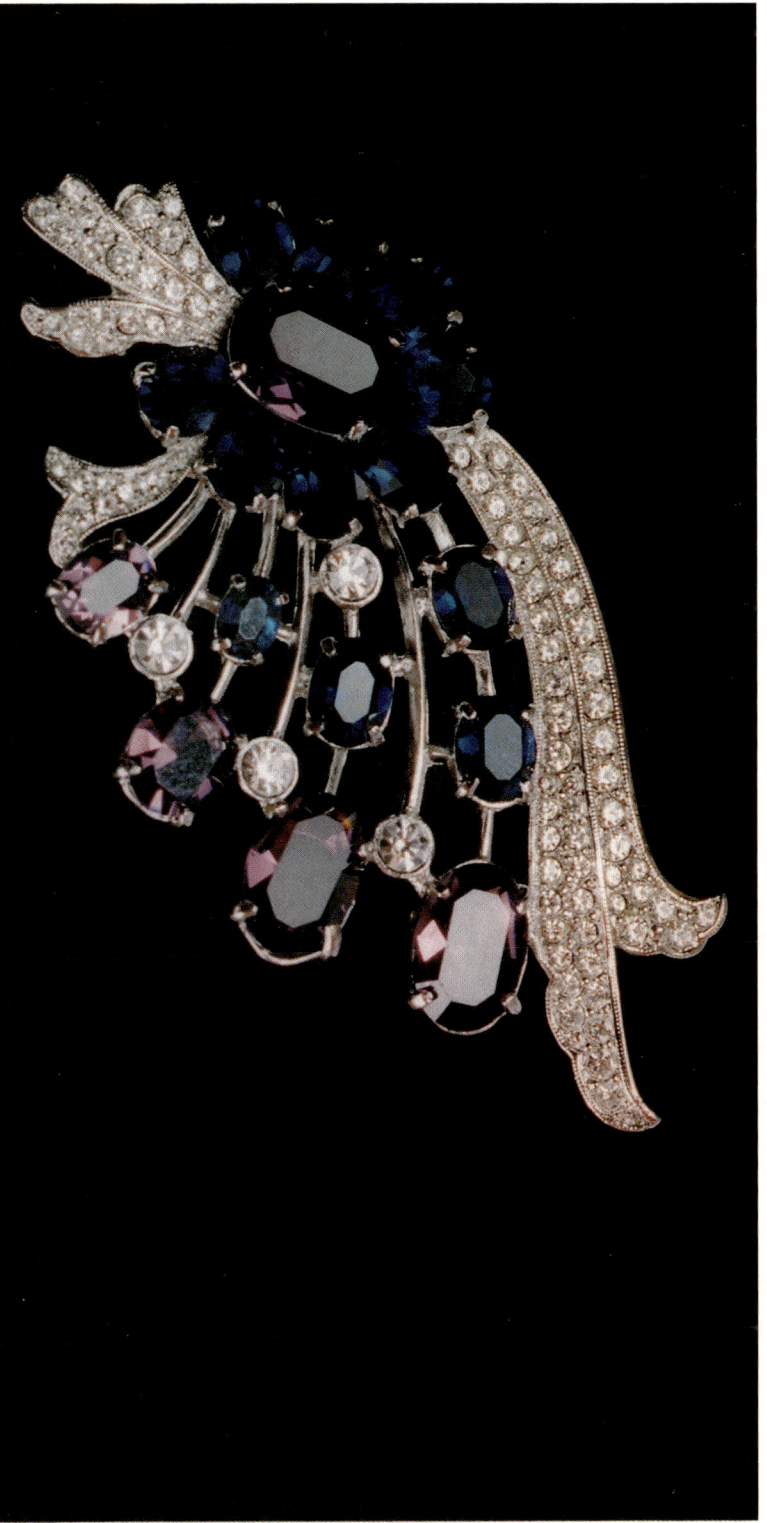

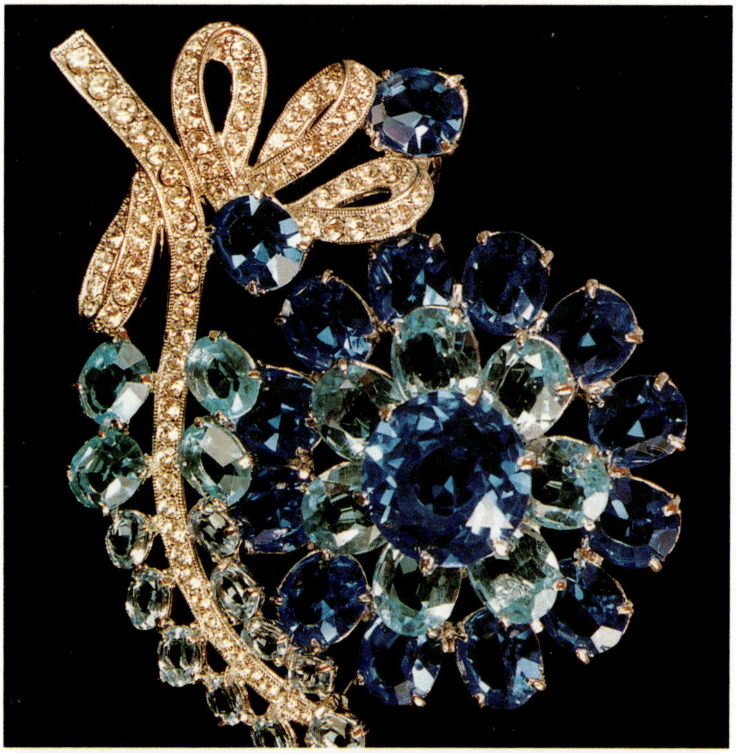
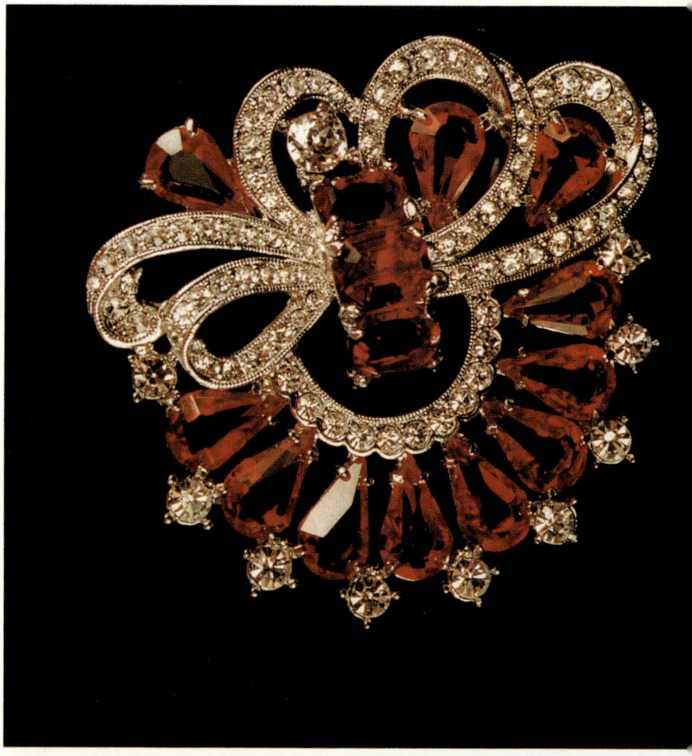
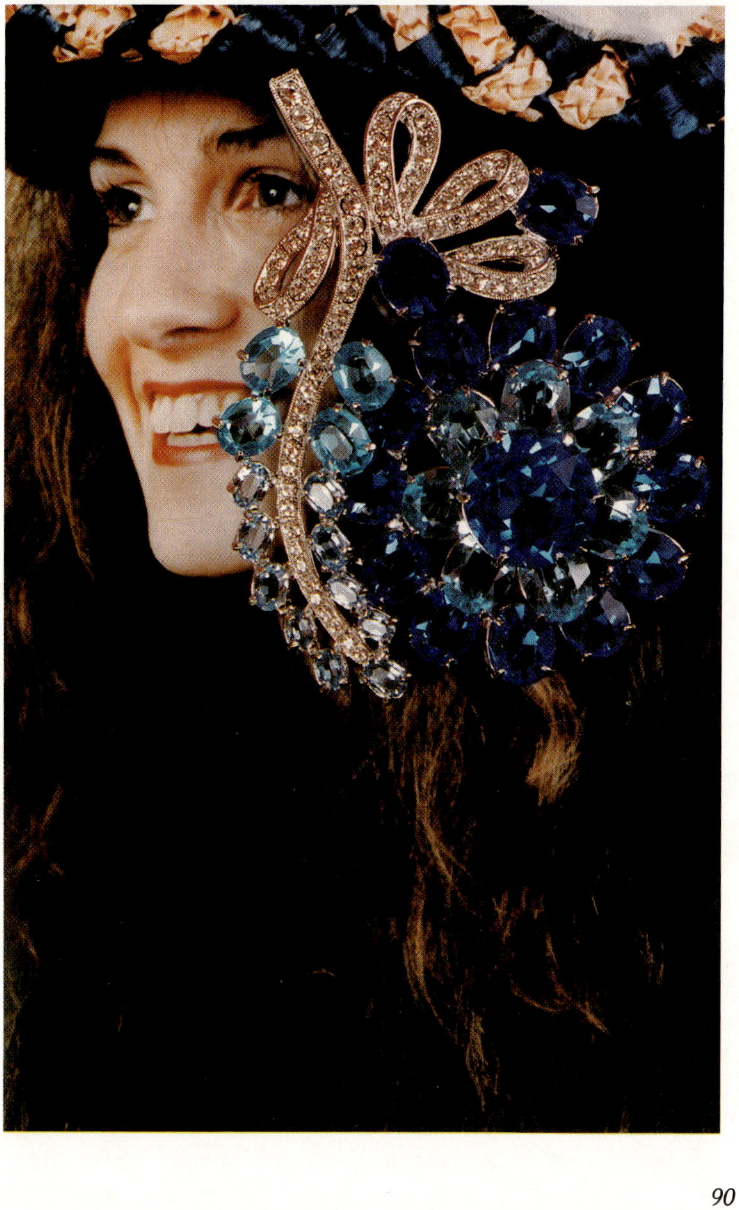
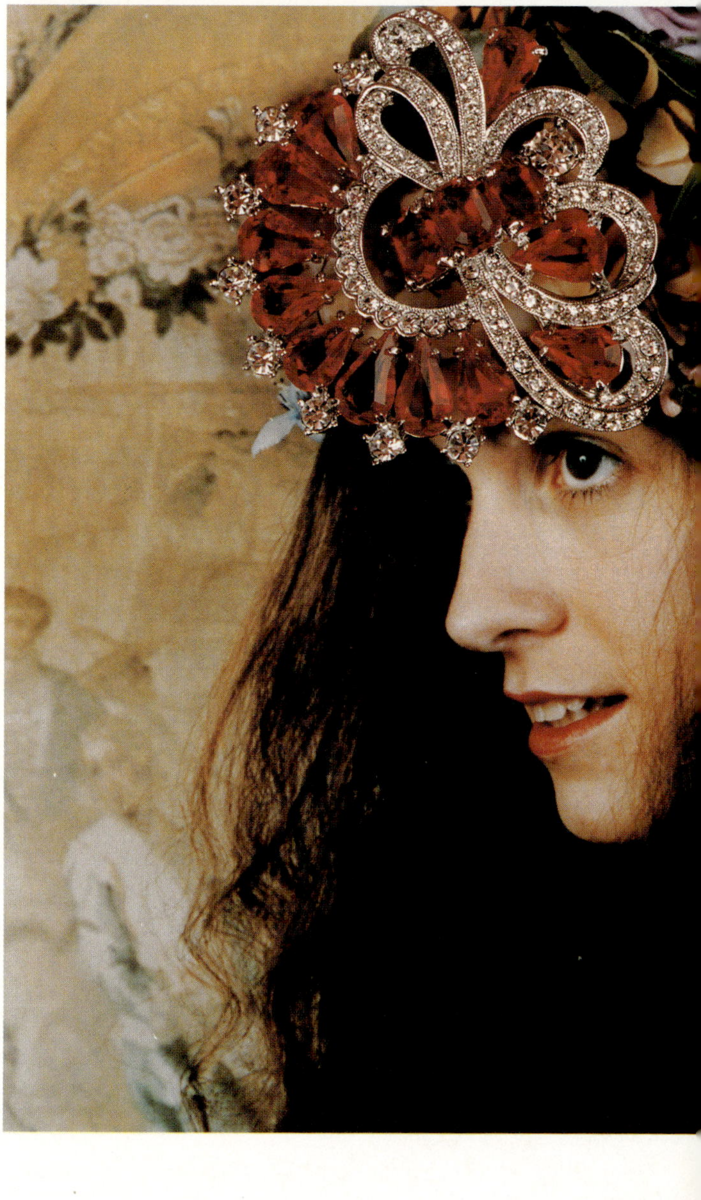

EUGENE

By Eugene...this multi-layered brooch in shades of midnight blue, silver, and coppery gold nestles comfortably in its "perch" amid two silver cranes.

FLORENZA

A master designer, Dan Kasoff was the owner and guiding force behind Florenza. Based on 28th Street in New York City, Florenza was in business from the 1940s until it ceased operations in 1981. Assisted by his son Larry, Kasoff produced many fine pieces that incorporated intricate stone work and detail reminiscent of antique Victorian designs, a timeless look that invariably rises above the vagaries of time and fashion.

This blackamoor stickpin artfully combines the many elements for which Florenza is noted–interesting designs, superb casting, unusual stones, and appealing antiqued finish.

Florenza bracelet with an Oriental look and unusual, intertwining gold frame.

The key to your heart...a gold angel sits atop a key entwined with a rope of beading on this whimsical brooch by Florenza.

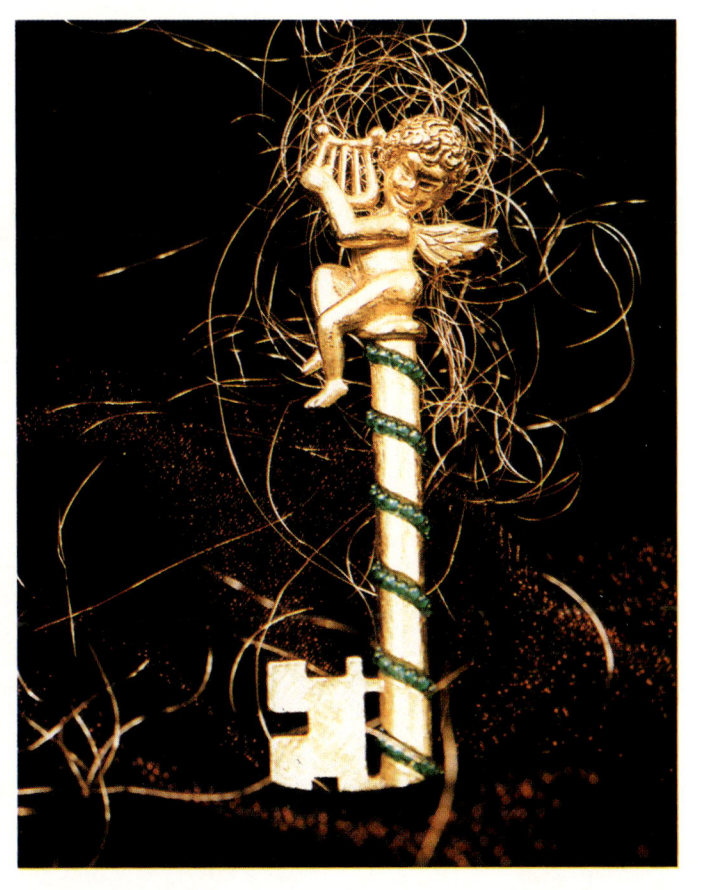

Of more recent vintage, multi-colored composition hearts in a bold and colorful Givenchy necklace.

GIVENCHY

A couturier who worked initially with fashion giants like Fath and Lelong, and also designed for Schiaparelli, Huburt de Givenchy was only 24 years of age when he opened his own couture house in 1952. In 1957 he introduced the first of many Givenchy fragrances, later following with jewelry and other accessories.

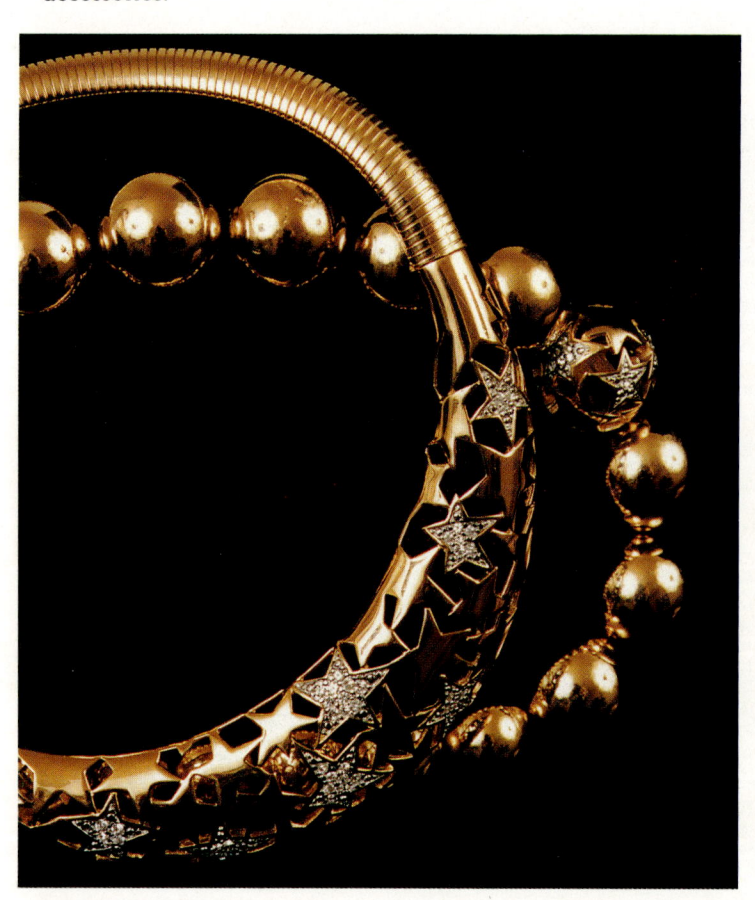

A celestial Givenchy collar and metal bead choker.

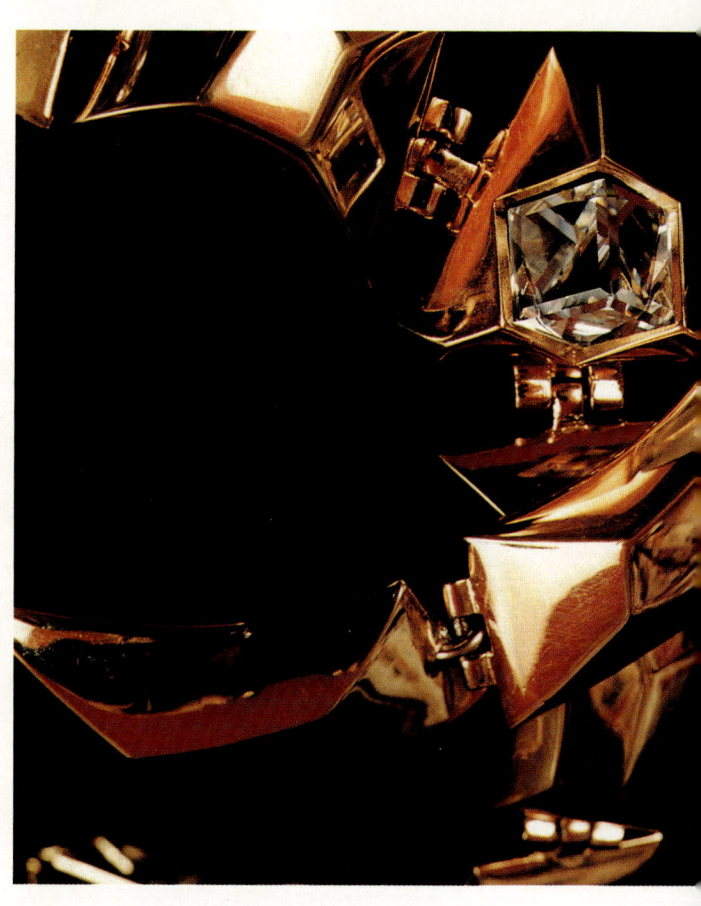

This massive Givenchy necklace has large three-dimensional links, accented with huge faceted crystals.

LEO GLASS

Named after its founder and guiding force, the Leo Glass Company of New York brought high-quality costume jewelry pieces to the public from 1943 to 1957. Not found with much frequency, the elegant and unusual designs of pieces marked "Leo Glass" make them well worth the search.

Hundreds of findings with antiqued gold finishes combine with coral glass beads in this necklace by Leo Glass.

By Leo Glass, a beautifully designed brooch with odd-shaped center stone, accented with regal purple enamel, violet stones, and pave rhinestones.

HAR

Marked HAR, this necklace is a masterful combination of golden mesh and an unusual pendant of large faux mabe pearls and purple iridescents, all with an unusual 3-D cut and each overlapped with delicate gold ferns. Note the unusual clasp of brushed gold, centered with a single stone.

MIRIAM HASKELL

With the resurgence of interest in vintage costume jewelry, the story of Miriam Haskell has, by now, become a familiar one. Here was a creative individual who was "ahead of her time" and motivated by the desire to offer carefully-constructed jewelry in intricate yet bold designs. Courageously venturing into uncharted territory, her success was phenomenal, and vintage Haskell pieces remain among the most popular and sought after today, each one offering a new visual adventure.

After World War II, the renowned Haskell pearls came from a small glass manufacturer in Japan. All were hand made, even the seed pearls, with the magnificent baroque pearls supplied to Haskell exclusively. The Haskell operation consistently used the back-stringing method then employed in fine jewelry. Bearing in mind that pinbacks can, of course, break and be replaced, one clue to an authentic Haskell creation from this period is the pinback, which will never fold back more than 1/2 or 3/4 of the way.

In 1954, Morris Kinsler bought the original Haskell business from Haskell's brother, who had managed it prior to and following her death in 1981, with Frank Hess continuing as the major designer. In 1984, Kinzler sold the business to Sanford Moss, who continued to manufacture jewelry in the same Haskell tradition, including the importation of all findings and stampings from centuries-old European manufacturers.

In 1990, the business was sold to Frank Fialkoff and, under the name Haskell Jewels Ltd., beautiful jewelry continues to be produced in much the same fashion as the earlier lines. All pieces are still hand set, with many boasting an antique Russian gold finish in the tradition of Haskell's fine vintage designs.

"Charming"! To wrap 'round the wrist, this charm bracelet by Miriam Haskell is a joy from any angle.

Worth a second look! These close-ups show the intricate detail on a large Haskell brooch, which rises, layer upon layer, to its spectacular center. A crowning tribute to the glory of Haskell.

A monumental Miriam Haskell brooch in pink marbleized stones of unusual shape, offset by clusters of seed pearls, pink glass beads, and a giant pearl.

Large circular discs of seed pearls make this beautiful necklace and earrings parure by Miriam Haskell both unique and dramatic.

Like ropes of luminescent flying saucers, pictured here is a section of a triple-strand Mirian Haskell necklace.

Whether worn horizontally or vertically, this towering giant is pure Haskell!

Here we see Haskell's trademark pearls and mirrorbacks interestingly combined with pastel stones of various sizes and hues.

Measuring 2", with its antique feather, sparkling crystals, nacreous shell and single pearl, this Haskell design is the ultimate in beauty and grace of line.

All of the same genre, Miriam Haskell brooches to gladden any collector's heart!

97

Hundreds of seed pearls create a free-form 1.5" cluster in this Haskell brooch with antique gold leaf and mabe pearl center.

A green center stone sets the tone for this unusual Haskell brooch.

The epitome of sophistication by Miriam Haskell–shimmering strands of crystals and pearls topped by giant pink stones and seed pearls in this bracelet and earrings parure.

The many faces of Miriam Haskell...necklaces, bracelets, and earrings featuring mirrorbacks, mabe pearls, seed pearls, and glittering crystals.

HOBÉ

Highly regarded by their peers through four generations of Old World craftsmen, the Hobe family has been providing stunning, imaginative designs to the public since Jacque Hobé supplied costume jewelry with a "fine jewelry" look for the Parisienne social set of 1887. Early in this century, his son William brought this well-honed talent to the United States with glorious results, in turn passing them along to his sons Robert and Donald. Never stinting on craftsmanship and quality, their lines throughout the ensuing years offered only the finest in costume pieces in a wide array of versatile designs—each line standing apart from the last.

Robert's son Jim, an able designer in his own right, continues the family tradition from his studio in Rhode Island.

The glory of Hobé!

Cigarette cases from Hobé's 1940's "Madonna Collection." Featuring genuine carved jade and coral, crystal, ruby, and jonquil dentelles, each stone was individually hand set into a filigree interweave. Note how the interplay of stones on the multi-colored case was artfully designed to focus the eye on the jade ovals. Each of these cases was limited to 150 pieces.

Limited also to only 30 pieces, shown here is a rectangular Hobé jewel case, with close up of cover. Circa early 1950s.

With the ambiance of a Victorian heirloom, another Hobé design.

With hard-fired enameling, emphasized by genuine cultured pearls, delicate ruby dentelles, and Russian gold finish, this brooch is indicative of the skills involved in producing Hobé's 1960's "Old World Art" collection.

With over 400 individually hand-set stones, and centered with a miniature of the Empress Eugenie, a jewel box by Hobe from their Empress Eugenie collection, circa early 1950s. A limited edition treasure, only 30 pieces were produced.

From the Empress Eugenie collection, a pear-shaped brooch accentuated with filigree wire work centering each of the hand set rose, crystal, and ruby dentelles.

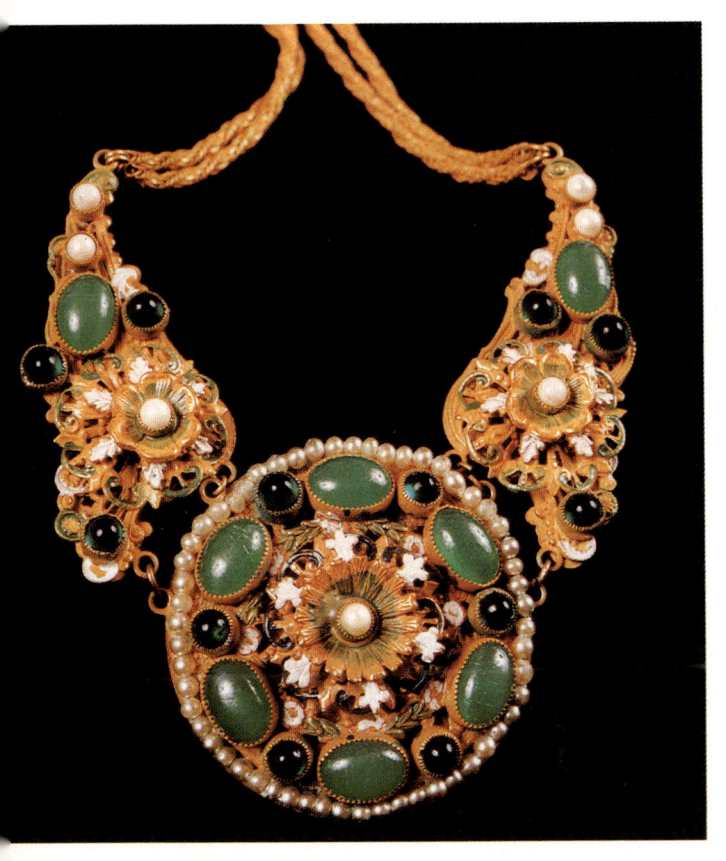

Also from Hobe's "Old World Art" collection, a dynamic necklace in Russian gold finish, its regal look emphasized by the contrast of cultured pearls and enamel to the jade and emerald cabochons.

Courtesy of the private collection of Robert and James Hobe.

From Hobé's Ming collection of the 1950s, a lovely example of a "good luck" Oriental face carving surrounded with hand set, multi-colored dentelles, each in its own bezel setting with filigree woven wire emphasis.

A Hobé brooch awash with its colorful African heritage; the charming face is surrounded by flowers, stones, and tassels.

An intricate, Renaissance-inspired Hobé necklace.

Sterling by Hobé. The variety of designs in this popular Hobé line never ceases to amaze!

Oriental magic by Hobé...carved composition ivory figural brooch with giant headdress encased in gold filigree and studded with stones.

Part of a Hobé necklace/bracelet parure, this close-up of the bracelet reveals the seemingly random placement of the hand-set stones—a design that was far from "random," requiring patience and skill to execute.

A Hobé classic, this sterling flower is a symphony of design and color.

Hobé sterling, both of similar design, but each uniquely different.

106

HOLLYCRAFT

Hollycraft's founder was Joseph Chorbajian, born in Marash, Turkey in 1900. He survived the Turkish massacre of 1915 and came to the U.S. in 1917.

Chorbajian founded Hollycraft in the early 1940s, in partnership with Jack Hazard and his cousin Archie. Originally at 902 Broadway in New York City, the business was later moved to 37th Street, and in 1972 was sold, continuing for only a few years thereafter. Joseph Chorbajian died in 1991 at the age of 91.

Hollycraft remains one of the most desired vintage jewelry collectibles, inevitably attracting attention for their finely-crafted designs that reflect the beauty of centuries past. Many were in an appealing melange of pastel stones, a combination that has since become its hallmark. Hollycraft designs are particularly attractive to collectors, not only for their visual appeal, but also for their general affordability when weighing quality against cost.

A melange of pieces created by Dorothy Torem from original photographs of old Hollycraft designs. Courtesy of Joyce Chorbajian.

Rarely seen...this duette is signed Hollycraft.

In a somewhat larger design than usually found in Hollycraft pieces, this necklace of faux blue topaz, tiny pearls, and slinky snake chain still maintains its dainty, Victorian-style appeal.

ISADORA

Home for the holidays! A Hollycraft Christmas tree brooch.

From the 1960s and marked Isadora, a whimsical composition necklace with a sad-faced Pierrot pendant at its center.

JEANNE

Always offering figural designs that are finely crafted and designed, this Jeanne elephant is no exception.

JOSEFF OF HOLLYWOOD

Wearing a necklace by Joseff, the beauteous Linda Darnell was bejeweled and bewitching in this film still from "Forever Amber."

All Joseff movie photographs and jewelry courtesy of Joan Castle Joseff

Take an illustrious heritage, surround it with fantasy and glamour, mix with a sense of wonder and nostalgia, and many of the ingredients necessary to create a "masterpiece" are already in place. Jewels by Joseff of Hollywood qualify on every count. Responsible for over ninety-five percent of the jewelry seen in America's favorite films during the late 1930s, '40s, and '50s (and on that basis alone, standing uniquely apart), his contributions to the industry thus need no introduction. Eugene Joseff's offerings graced the neck of Vivien Leigh's Scarlett in "Gone With the Wind," Greta Garbo donned his creations in "Camille," and they enhanced the regality of Norma Shearer in "Marie Antoinette" and Bette Davis in "Elizabeth and Essex"...the list goes on and on. Without exception, the movie jewelry was provided to the studio on a lease basis and never sold to them or to the public.

Recognizing the potential appeal of pieces of similar style, Joseff had the foresight to also offer the public a retail line that mirrored the look of many of his exotic movie offerings. During the 1940s and Fifties, this Joseff jewelry was available at only one store or boutique in each major U.S. city. It is these vintage pieces, and others assembled from the old findings, that are being collected today. Older Joseff retail pieces (circa 1930s, '40s), are marked "Joseff-Hollywood" and shortly thereafter inscribed simply with the name "Joseff." All are highly collectible. Buyers should be cautious, however, of any claim that the piece being offered for sale is one-of-a-kind or from a Hollywood movie, since this is most unlikely.

Joseff designs reflect the glamour and mystique to be found in America's "golden age" of movies. Their sheer eye appeal creates immediate interest (regardless of whether the viewer has any previous knowledge of Joseff), making them unique in the designer costume jewelry field, and providing the Joseff legacy with a special and unique niche in its history.

Following his untimely death in 1948, the several million-plus pieces of movie jewelry from that era and later have rested safely in the archives of Joan Castle Joseff–Eugene Joseff's widow–who remains the guiding force behind Joseff enterprises to the present time.

Joseff's famous "Queen for a Day" crown.

Shirley MacLaine and David Niven in "Around the World in 80 Days." The pearl, rhinestone-capped choker is by Joseff.

Irene Hervey and the debonair William Powell in the 1948 Universal film "Mr. Peabody and the Mermaid." Joseff's brooch also converts to a pendant.

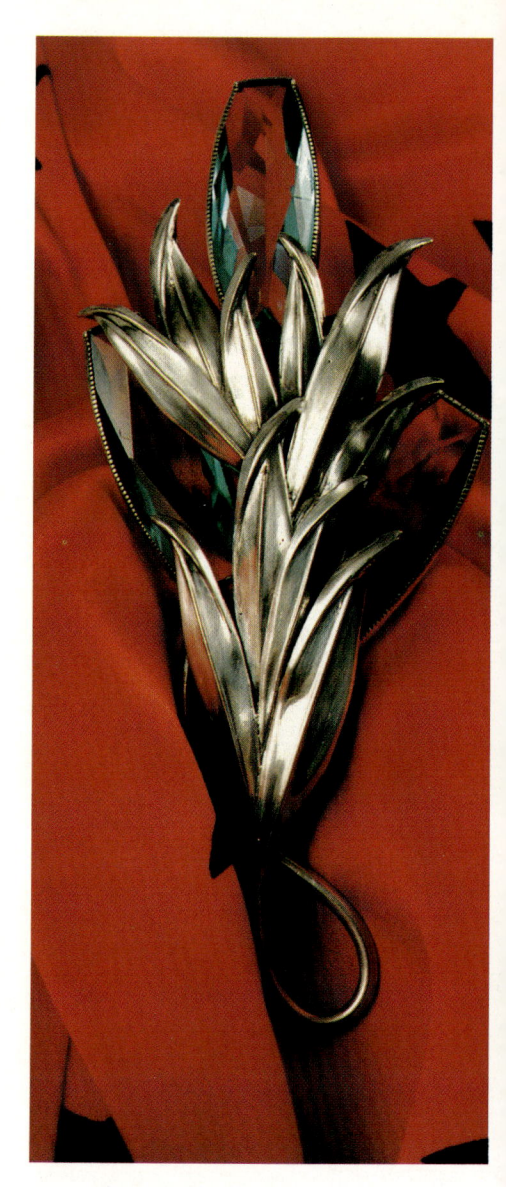

Signed Joseff-Hollywood, this 1940s sterling brooch is from his early retail line. Towering 5", it features large, rectangular-shaped faux aquamarine stones in a beaded setting.

A breathtaking shot of titian-haired Ann Sheridan. The movie was Warner Bros.' "The Patient in Room 18."

Marked Joseff Hollywood, an amethyst-centered flower from the retail line.

112

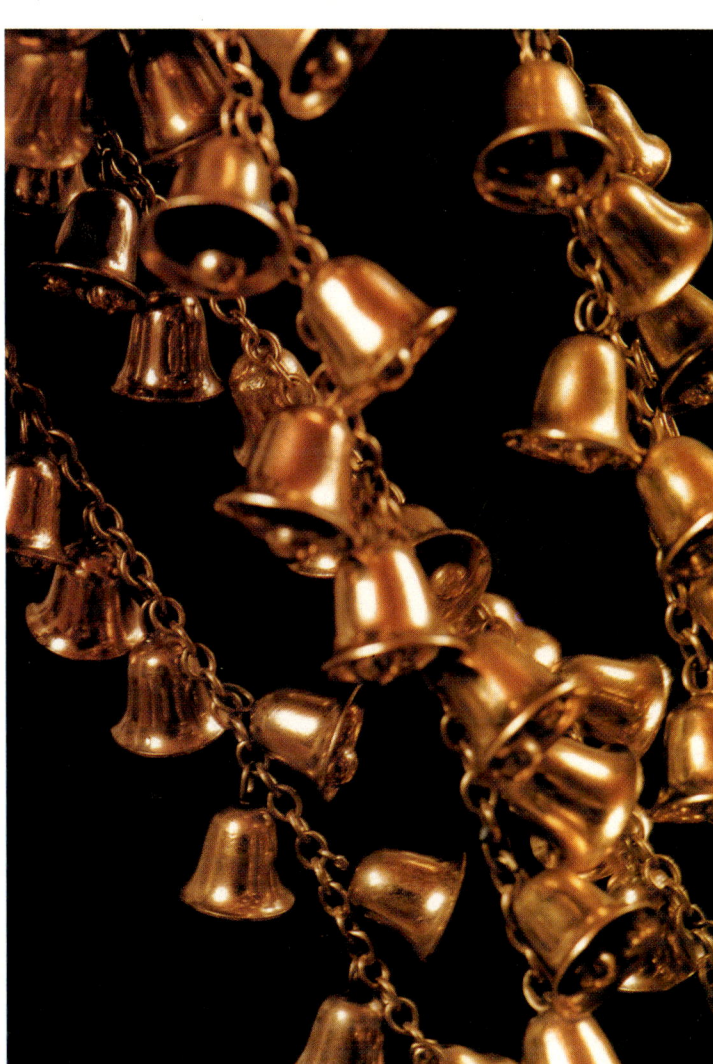

Ring those bells! Twined time and again around the neck, each of these, numbering an unbelievable 125, has its own clapper. A particular favorite of Joan Crawford, this cacophony of tinkling bells was destined to make an audible fashion statement.

Marked Joseff Hollywood, a large, domed retail piece in sterling silver.

Twin bracelets of exquisite proportions and detail, worn in tandem by Genevieve Tobin in the 1937 film "The Great Gambini."

114

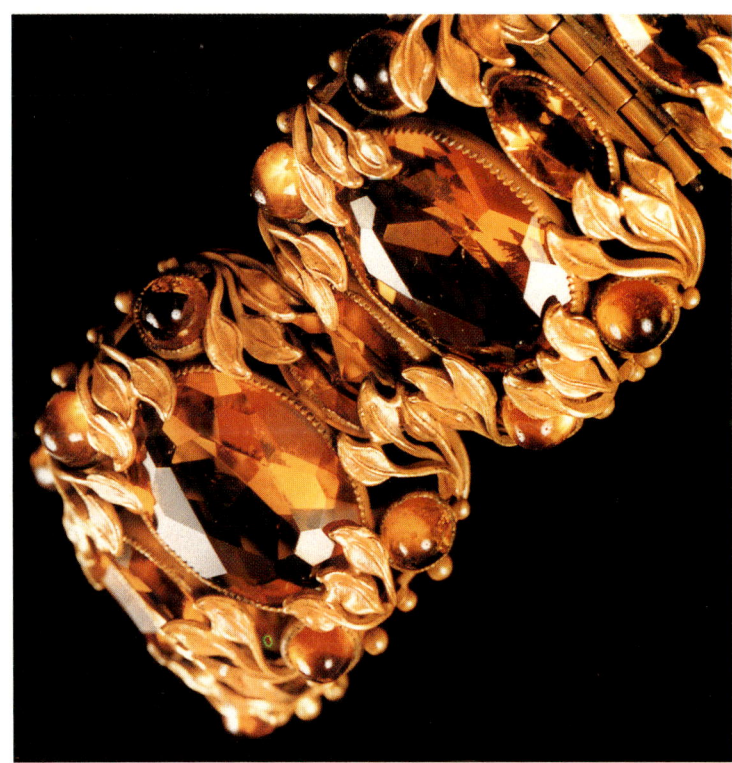

Topaz splendor! This bracelet clasped Greer Garson's wrist in "Random Harvest."

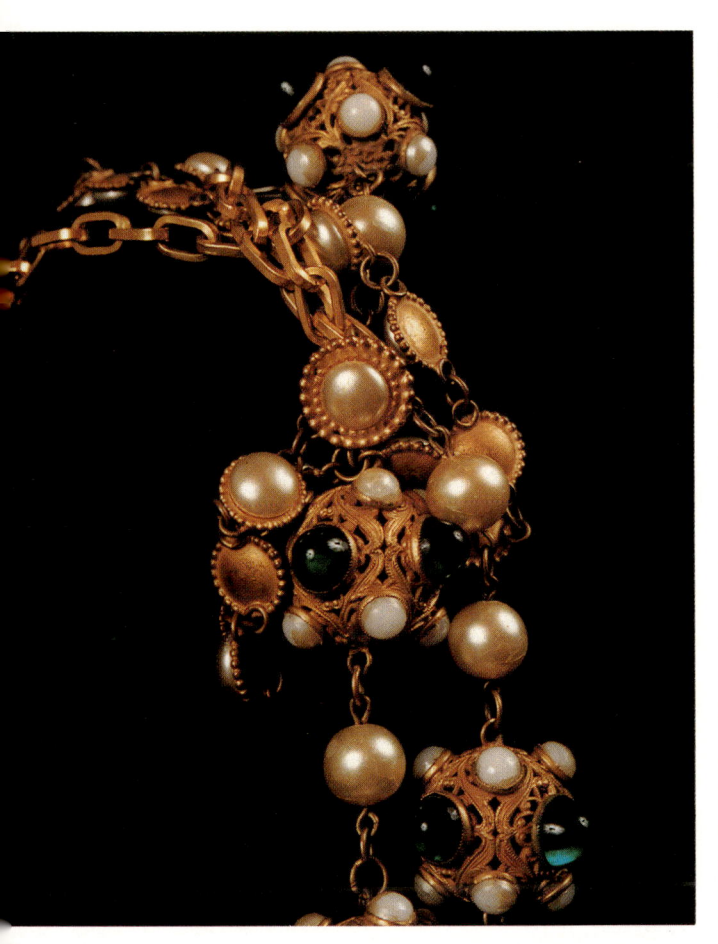

This gold and pearl order chain with jeweled filigree balls hung majestically from the waist of Barbara O'Neil, who portrayed Queen Elizabeth in Universal's 1937 "Tower of London."

115

Upper arm bracelet, worn seductively by Jody Lawrence in this movie still from 1951's "Ten Tall Men"; her co-star was Burt Lancaster.

The actress, Shelley Winters; the movie "South Seas Sinner," circa 1939; her companion, MacDonald Carey; the necklace, Joseff.

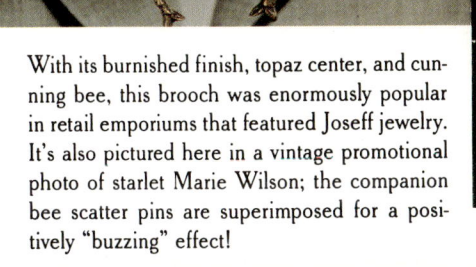

With its burnished finish, topaz center, and cunning bee, this brooch was enormously popular in retail emporiums that featured Joseff jewelry. It's also pictured here in a vintage promotional photo of starlet Marie Wilson; the companion bee scatter pins are superimposed for a positively "buzzing" effect!

From the Joseff retail line, a floral cuff bracelet and matching amethyst-centered brooch.

By Joseff, a burnished metal and clear faux aquamarine crystals in bezeled settings. Its companion, in sterling silver, is also shown.

117

KORDA

Inspired by the 1940 movie, pieces from "The Thief of Bagdad" jewelry series by producer Alexander Korda...a cuff bracelet and a "magic genie" brooch replete with scimitars and Aladdin slippers are in sharp contrast to the burnished leopard waiting for his prey.

Looking like something from "The Arabian Nights," a colorful "Thief of Bagdad" pendant by Korda.

KRAMER

Under the aegis of the three Kramer brothers, Louis, Morris, and Harry, the Kramer jewelry operation was founded in 1943. Marked "Kramer" or "Kramer of New York," they also contributed to the Dior line during the 1950s, with these particular items then marked "Dior by Kramer." Ceasing operations in the late 1970s, Kramer also fell victim to the vagaries of the costume jewelry market during that tumultuous time.

Fit for a Medieval castle, this hefty 3" brooch/pendant by Kramer is indicative of the overall care and quality that went into its manufacture, including the heavy, carefully plated and polished gold backing.

A combination of pewter-toned backing, metal loops, and brilliant stones form the basis for this unusual bracelet by Kramer of New York.

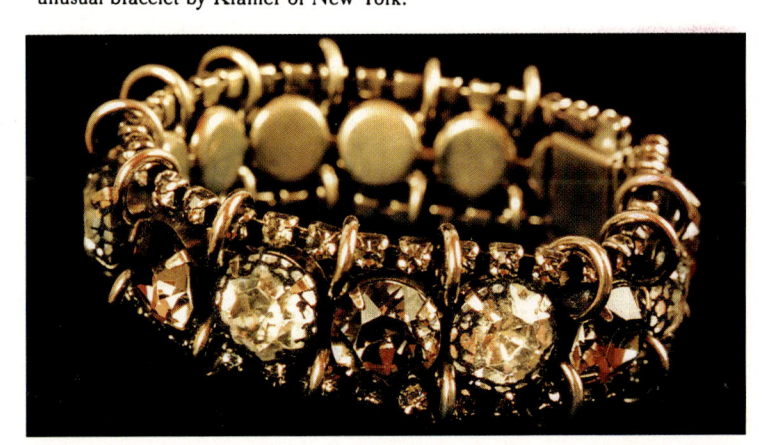

A tower of power...an intriguing combination of pale blue and purple, this brooch, necklace, bracelet, and earrings are marked "By Kramer for Dior."

This 2.75" Kramer beauty has overlapping open circles surrounding a large emerald green stone.

A delightful Kramer bracelet with matching earrings. Note the variety of stones, from opalescents and iridescents to delicately carved ones, all in soft, complementary shades.

KENNETH JAY LANE

The name Kenneth Jay Lane has become an almost generic one for costume jewelry. An elegant fixture in the industry since 1963, he has consistently offered a vast array of unusual designs, many of which had their origins in fine jewelry's greatest moments. They have been inspired by such diverse periods as the Ancient and Medieval, as well as the modernistic stylings of Art Deco. Seemingly never at a loss for new directions, Kenneth Jay Lane continues to reign as a costume jewelry icon. With his name perhaps better known to the general public than most (a credit not only to the appeal of his wide-ranging designs but also to his marketing genius), his jewelry inevitably commands attention and is always in great demand.

Not a brooch, but easily converted to one, this KJL buckle of hammered gold features a three-dimensional leopard leaping through the center. Note the gracefully intertwined tail.

The Year of the Dragon...a domed KJL brooch featuring turquoise and coral stones in deep mountings.

A KJL multi-strand pearl choker, focusing on the intertwined design of rhinestone encrusted petals on the giant clasp.

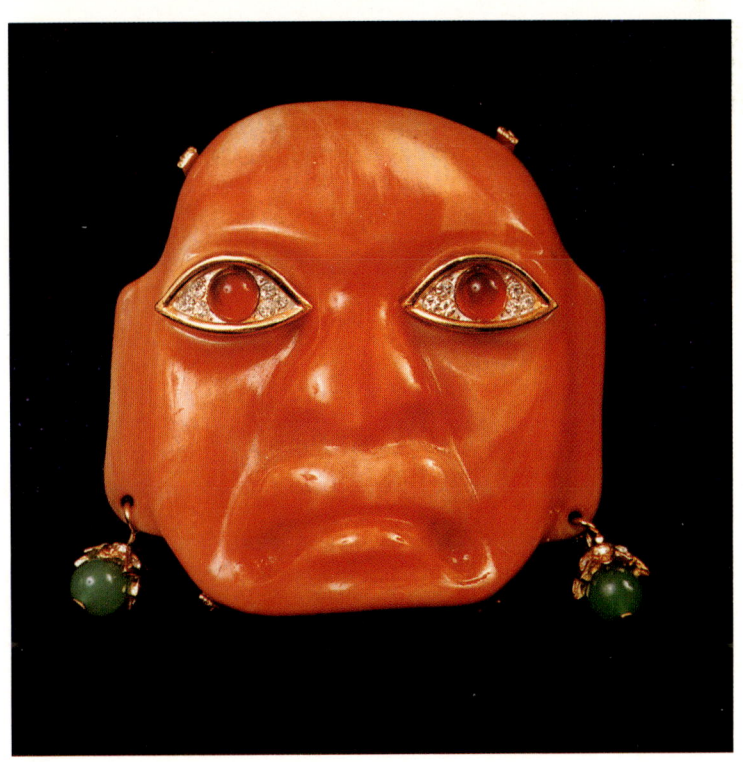

The bold and the beautiful...a primitive face by KJL.

121

On a long, supple rope with the look of braided gold, this enormous pendant is by KJL. The open, three-dimension effect gives added impetus to a monumental piece.

Of the same design genre, a cuff of marbleized composition with rhinestone accents and earrings rimmed with black enamel. Both marked Kenneth Lane.

122

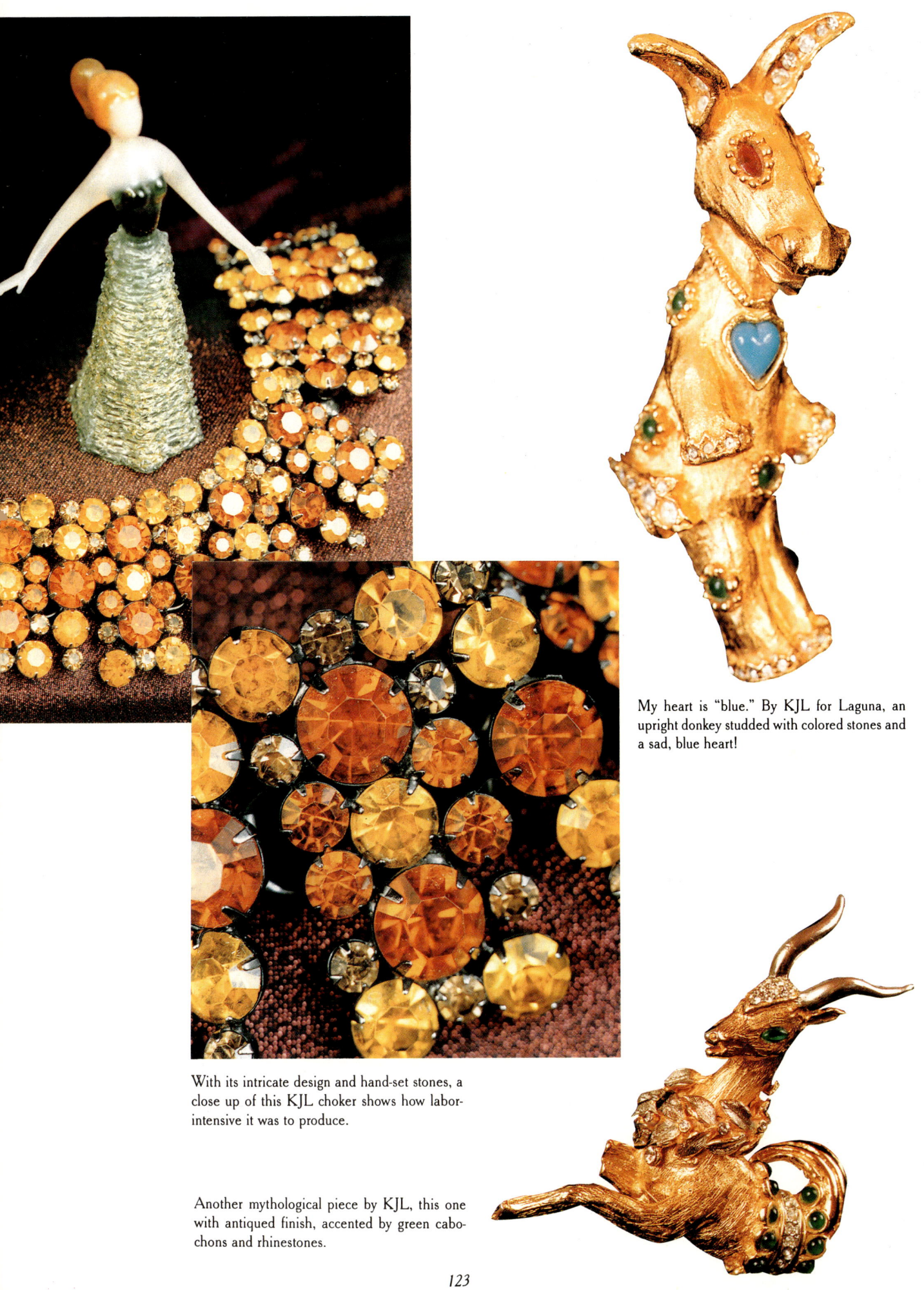

My heart is "blue." By KJL for Laguna, an upright donkey studded with colored stones and a sad, blue heart!

With its intricate design and hand-set stones, a close up of this KJL choker shows how labor-intensive it was to produce.

Another mythological piece by KJL, this one with antiqued finish, accented by green cabochons and rhinestones.

From the late 16th century, the Canning jewel, which became the inspiration for many ornate and cleverly executed costume jewelry designs of the 20th century.

In the style of the late sixteenth century Italian Renaissance "Canning Jewel," a pendant currently on display in the Victoria and Albert Museum in London (and purchased by them in 1935 for $26,000 U.S.), this 3" KJL for Laguna brooch, with nacreous breastplate, pave and enamel "tail," and dangling pearls, captures an ancient look in modern times. Similar designs were very popular during the Italian Renaissance, all combining fantasy figures and usually with three or more pearls dangling from the bottom, which served to balance the design. The "Canning Jewel" is a glorious riot of colorful enamel and sparkling stones and pearls. Centuries later, KJL once again brought this delightful look into twentieth century costume jewelry. Topping the frame of this "masterpiece" is a 3.75" unsigned bow brooch of pink moonstones and crystals, accented by faux amethysts.

Framed...again, in the mythological mode, this KJL piece is also balanced by three pearls, as was done in the sixteenth century.

Sir Lancelot, perhaps? This "knight rider" is by KJL.

LEIBER, LES BERNARD, AND VOGUE

The majority of the Vogue and Les Bernard pieces shown here are original showroom samples from the 1960s. Vogue was founded by Harold Shapiro and two other partners in 1936. The Shapiro family ended their association with Vogue in 1962; however, the Vogue name continued until the mid-1970s. Following in the family tradition, Bernard Shapiro, Harold's son, founded the Les Bernard operation in 1963.

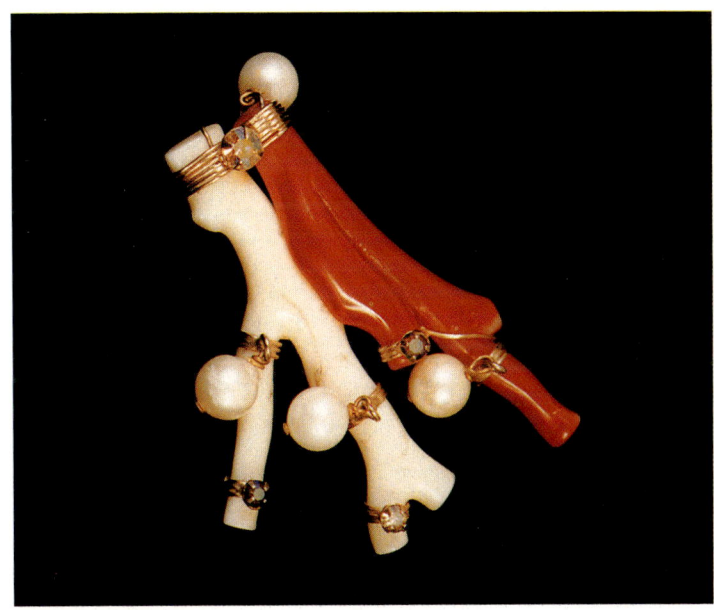

This genuine white and orange branch coral brooch was given added impetus by incorporating cultured pearls and rhinestones to its design. By Vogue, circa late 1940s, all pieces were wired by hand, with no two exactly alike.

Massive in weight and size, two brooch/pendants by Judith Leiber of handbag fame. Trained in the European guild tradition, Leiber's jewelry reflects the same meticulous care as her handbags, which have achieved "works of art" status.

First introduced by Vogue in the early 1940s, and then in the Les Bernard pieces pictured, these marcasite pins represent the first time ever that genuine marcasites were combined with colored stones, and also the first time marcasites were shown on gold plating as opposed to traditional silver (which accounts for the soft coppery hue of the marcasites). Since the settings for genuine marcasite and colored stones are different (rhinestones have pointed backs; marcasites flat ones), the models required intense "layout work," all of which was done by Bernard Shapiro's master partner, Lester Joy (hence, the name "Les Bernard").

Jewelry courtesy of Bernard Shapiro.

A Vogue creation, this three-strand, faux fresh water pearl, hand-knotted necklace is particularly unique because of its intricate, semi-precious clasp, shown here in detail. Every clasp was handmade to fit the varying shapes and sizes of the semi-precious stones, so no two were exactly alike. Clio Novelties, a Brooklyn-based manufacturer of quality domestic glass beads, supplied the Vogue pearls.

Circa early 1970s, these vermeil pins have special "Diamond Point Texture" (a registered trademark of Les Bernard). The texture was created by a diamond-pointed tool that was hand applied to every piece; the stones are genuine rubies.

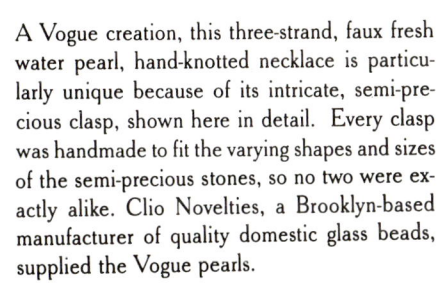

Les Bernard was a pioneer in jewelry designs featuring rhinestones with marcasites. Whereas the backs of rhinestones are pointed, those of marcasites are flat. Consequently, working with them required intensive model-making, with different settings for each marcasite stone as opposed to the settings necessary for rhinestones. To mix the two obviously presented a very tedious, labor-intensive task, making these pieces far more involved to produce than they might, at first glance, appear.

From Les Bernard, circa 1968, a 40" gold and silverplated "silken thread" knotted necklace. Approximately 84 feet of chain was used to make this twenty-four strand necklace. Can you imagine the worker holding all that chain while creating nine properly-spaced chain knots? Also note the use of the barrel screw clasp, with a hole punched through so all beads and chains could be identified.

Golden-hued marcasites by Vogue and Les Bernard represent the first lines by any manufacturer that combined marcasites with gold-backed designs, giving the pieces a warm, coppery glow.

Although Bernard Shapiro remains an active participant in today's Les Bernard operation, the company is now managed by another owner.

A delightful combination of strategically placed miniature cabochons are studded sparingly on this paved rhinestone cuff bracelet by Les Bernard.

By Ledo. A wide bracelet with bold, openwork links accented by giant, emerald green "jelly" stones.

With giant stones encased in a woven, basketlike casting, shown here is the center section of a six-strand necklace by Vogue.

This Ledo design has three interconnected areas of interest, and features an openwork rhinestone design, accented with two unusual wing-style emerald glass beads, with a swirling pave leaf behind.

Fashioned from the lightweight faux metal so often used following the shortages of World War II, this chunky but beautiful bracelet and earrings set by Lisner is from the 1950s.

LISNER

The japanned backing on this pair of Lisner brooches gives added impetus to the red stones. This style of black backing, particularly popular in the 1950s and '60s, not only provided an interesting contrast but was also very effective in heightening the color and clarity of the stones. Although much of their buisiness was as jobbers, Lisner produced an enormous quantity of pieces under their own name. They were eventually sold, and have not been in business for the last several decades.

129

MAZER

The Mazer family ventured into the manufacture of shoe buckles in the 1920s and then into the jewelry business; the Jomaz designation (for Joseph Mazer) later became a separate entity from the original Mazer operation.

The beauty of this close-up of a faux sapphire/diamond bracelet by Mazer speaks volumes. Of the same genre are the brooch and matching earrings by Jomaz.

An enormous 3" x 2", this swedged, dual-sectioned Mazer brooch has coral stones in a surrealistic design.

The subtle shading and blending of materials add much to the beauty of this 3.25" x 3" Monet fan brooch, with its delicate vaseline composition center and pink gold florentine rim that resembles golden wood.

MONET

Founded in 1937 by Jay and Michael Chernow, Monet had its beginnings in another specialized field of accessories–providing monograms for the handbag industry. Recognizing the emerging importance of costume jewelry, Monet entered that field shortly thereafter. Always moving with the ever-changing proclivities of a fickle public, they inherently understood that costume jewelry designs must be ever vigilant to fashion changes, a philosophy that has held them in good stead into the 1990s. Now a part of the Crystal Brands Jewelry Group (which also includes Trifari), Monet continues to supply mass market designs to major department stores throughout the United States.

NAPIER

Founded in 1875 as Whitncy and Rice in North Attleboro, Massachusetts, Napier later moved their operation to Meriden, Connecticut, where it remains today. Napier is the oldest costume jewelry company in the United States, still offering a broad range of mass-market lines in major department stores throughout the country. Their designs from the early and middle decades of this century, and most prominently those in sterling, are particularly noteworthy to today's collectors.

By Napier, a large sterling bow in a modernistic design, offset by a large milky-hued amethyst stone.

In a "monarch" 5" x 3.5" size, this Napier butterfly is free to flutter proudly on any lapel. Note the variations of gold tones and the filigree body.

Why gaze into the crystal ball when the treasure lies beneath? The Napier cuff with giant hammered gold links has milky amber stones dramatically encircling one end.

ORA

ORA was founded in Chicago in 1921 by Oreste Agnini, the first jewelry manufacturing operation to be established in that city. Born in Naples, Italy in 1885, Agnini displayed his artistic talents early. He studied at the Conservatory of Music in Naples and became an accomplished violinist, later achieving the position of concert master for the Wurlitzer Orchestra. Emigrating to the United States in 1903, Agnini served as an officer in the U.S. Air Force during World War I, and his drawing skills came to the fore as he hastily sketched his observations while behind enemy lines.

Agnini's partner in the jewelry manufacturing business was Ralph Singer, who handled the factory operation. Agnini devoted his time to jewelry design and general business responsibilities while his brother Hector oversaw the stone setting and packaging. Initially, the company was known as Agnini & Singer. All the stones used were Czechoslovakia and purchased in Rhode Island.

Measuring a mind-boggling 14 inches and covered with hand-set rhinestones, this is a replica of Charles A. Lindberg's airplane, fashioned by Oreste Agnini, founder of ORA designs. The original was sent to Anne Morrow Lindberg, and is now displayed in the Charles Lindberg Museum in Missouri. Courtesy of Nancy Agnini Brady.

It was Agnini & Singer who were responsible for supplying many of the buttons, pins, and brooches so coveted on Eisenberg dresses prior to the formation of the Eisenberg jewelry operation, and Agnini and Eisenberg remained friends for many years. A&S was also responsible for jewelry featuring the 1939 World's Fair symbol, as well as crowns for the Mardi Gras queens. With the growth of their business, they eventually maintained three showrooms in the United States–one in Chicago and the others in New York and San Francisco.

Early pieces of A&S jewelry had no stamping, and it is probable that many of the high quality, unsigned pieces displaying the delicate, Old World workmanship admired today are early examples of Oreste Agnini's work. Eventually the business was known as ORA Designs, and the ORA logo began appearing on the jewelry. In 1952, Agnini retired and sold his half of the business to Mr. Singer, who, along with his son-in-law, Raymond Pausback, then took over the design and manufacturing operations. The company ceased operations in the early 1960s.

The fine workmanship of Oreste Agnini is readily seen in these elegant yet delicate designs by ORA.

Sing for your supper...these birdies tweet happily in an ORA brooch replete with musical scales and crystal flowers! Courtesy of Nancy Agnini Brady.

All marked ORA, each pieces reflects the dainty and intricate designs for which Oreste Agnini was noted. Courtesy of Nancy Agnini Brady.

Moon over Miami...a special brooch created by Oreste Agnini for his wife. Courtesy of Nancy Agnini Brady.

PANETTA

Founded by Benedetto Panetta in 1945, who had previously worked as a model-maker for Trifari and later Pennino, Panetta jewelry has always been reflective of this impressive background. Blessed with a family lineage, Panetta's skills were carried on by his equally talented sons Amadeo and Armand, who continued the business until it was absorbed by a foreign buyer in the 1980s.

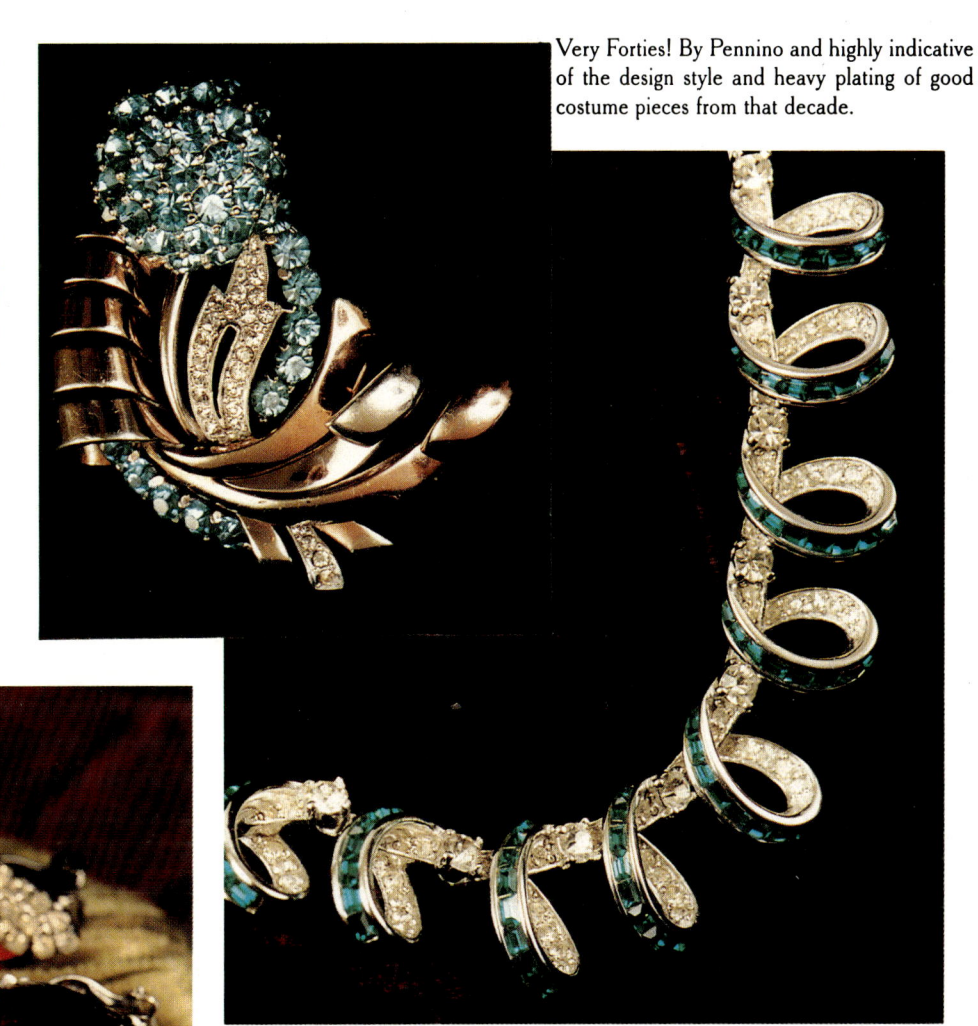

PENNINO

Very Forties! By Pennino and highly indicative of the design style and heavy plating of good costume pieces from that decade.

Portion of a delicately-intertwined Pennino necklace; matching screwback earrings. Circa 1940s.

A fish out of water–this one by Panetta has gold and enameled scales and rhinestone accents, and an unusual clip arrangement that converts it to a pendant.

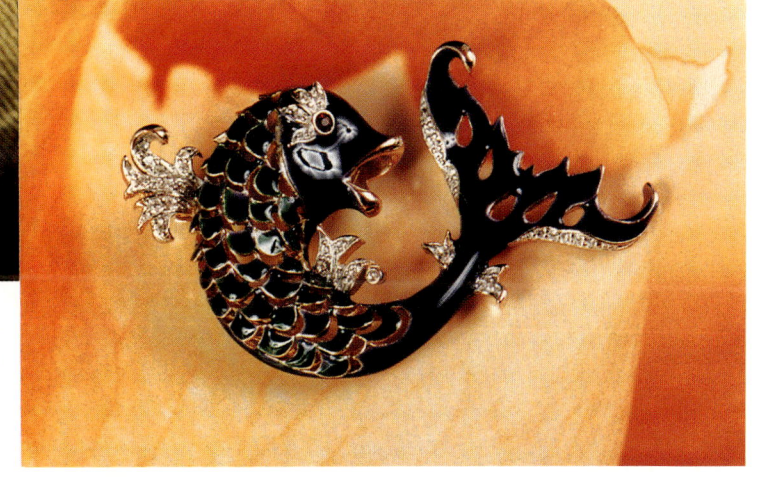

Become a "princess" when you pluck this dainty Panetta brooch and earrings parure from your jewelry case. It features rhinestone overlays capping brilliant garnet-red stones.

LUCIEN PICARD

Most prominently noted for their fine watches, the precision necessary for timepieces serves Lucien Picard well in this massive, finely-executed pendant with lapis accents.

Always exhibiting jewelry of distinction, Lucien Picard of timepiece fame produced this lavish bracelet and earrings set, replete with clusters of brilliant red stones encasing rows of glittering crystals.

PAULINE RADER

The daughter of a jewelry store owner, Pauline Rader began her career assisting in the construction and design of manipulated and custom-made pearl pieces. Preferring to express herself more independently, Rader established her own business in 1962, creating customized designs for private clients and boutique operations and never offering them to the public through the standard department store venue.

Many of Rader's innovative designs were prompted by her inherent attraction to antique jewelry, and she haunted antique shows and searched out unusual pieces during her many foreign travels. Coupled with historical research, fine jewelry designs that originating in places like Greece, Italy, and France were then converted by European craftsmen and Manhattan model makers to Rader's own costume interpretations, thus rooting many of her pieces in the mystique of ancient cultures. She was, in essence, the epitome of a conceptual artist. Finding them particularly adaptable to her personal style and taste, Rader was especially fond of incorporating turquoise, coral, and other semi-precious stones into her designs. Although Rader was assisted in the administrative areas of the business by her brother and sister-in-law, all designs marked "Pauline Rader" were solely her responsibility, making them more individualized than those of many of her contemporaries.

Surrounded by undulating rhinestone "waves," this "happy dolphin" by Pauline Rader has nacreous pale pink enamel and gold trim.

The complex techniques required for these gigantic pendants by Pauline Rader are easily apparent even to the untrained eye.

Lying in wait...a menacing alligator by Pauline Rader combines florentine gold finish with rhinestone-rimmed, red cabochon eyes and a spotted green enamel back.

"What kind of beast is this?" Pauline Rader interprets a particularly ferocious one, 3" in length, resplendent in shiny gold and white enamel.

A woodland sprite...playing the flutes of Pan, an "otherworldly" 3.25" brooch by Pauline Rader.

REGENCY

With an Old World look, this Regency parure combines antique silver with unusual grey pearls in a harmonious design of considerable detail.

REINAD

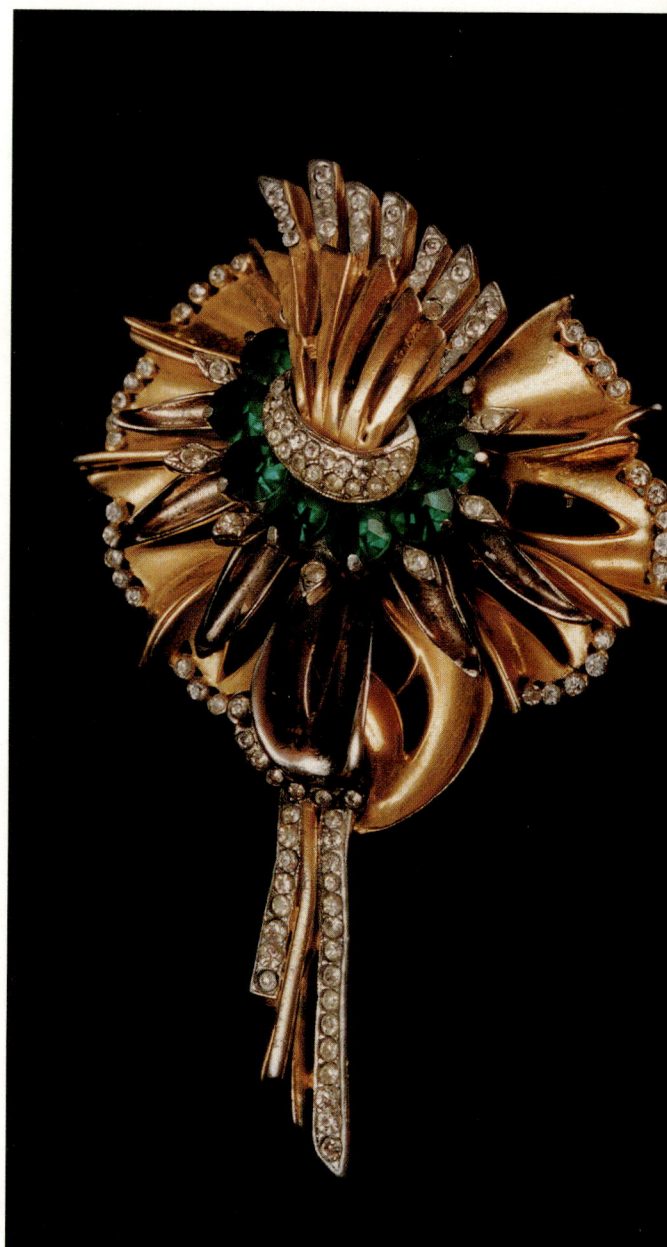

Heavily plated, a giant Reinad brooch that is a masterpiece of design and casting techniques.

REJA

This brooch by Reja is a symphony of graceful design and enameling skill. A beauty by any standards!

This same Reja brooch has found a "juicy" home on an antique flocked pear.

Offering designs of elegance and high quality, Reja was founded by Sol Finkelstein in the 1940s, with pieces sold primarily to boutiques and in relatively small quantities, accounting for their scarcity today. Uncover the name and a treasure goes with it! The company was disbanded in the 1960s.

ROBERT

What is now referred to as Robert jewelry had its beginnings in 1949. Originally called Fashioncraft, the name was changed to Robert Originals in 1960, taken from the name of Robert Levy, one of the original founders.

There are several bits of misinformation regarding Robert and Robert jewelry. Contrary to popular belief, Robert did not receive his training from Miriam Haskell nor did he ever work for that company. Often mispronounced, Robert is simply stated in the "good old American-style," minus the French flair. Nor is this Robert to be confused with Robert DeMario (another jewelry maven of the era); the two are not interchangeable, one having no relationship to the other.

A colorful character and design genius, Robert Levy retired in 1975, and the business was taken over by Ellen Jaffe, daughter of Robert Levy's partner, David Jaffe. The name changed to Ellen Designs, Inc. in 1984.

Like a Victorian masterpiece, the giant topaz stone in this Robert brooch is effectively "framed" in a braided golden oval with an inner band of tiny amber stones and antiqued "flowers" at each corner.

A melange of "heady" enameled brooches by Robert, all geared to the freshness and verve of 1950s and Sixties fashions.

By Robert, enameled cuffs that range from muted shades of shimmering caramels and greens, to brilliant reds, blues, and fuschias.

In a highly-polished enamel finish, a pair of charming butterflies by Robert.

By Robert. An enameled flower in autumn shades of gold, rust, and green.

141

The return of the Gothic...a gargoyle-inspired pendant by Robert.

With its unusual design reminiscent of Victorian times, these bezel-set stones on an intricate filigree base create a striking Robert brooch.

A departure from the look of most Robert designs, this jolly fellow, fashioned in sterling, could be a treasured companion.

Pearls among the seashells...A Robert design of antiqued gold, mirrorbacks, and large rhinestone-capped mabe pearls.

This stupendous Original by Robert is a mass of dangling pearls and crystals falling from antique gold leaves.

Robert unexcelled...a parure that reaches new heights with gold-capped pearls and an intricately wired center design.

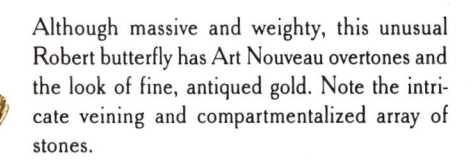

Although massive and weighty, this unusual Robert butterfly has Art Nouveau overtones and the look of fine, antiqued gold. Note the intricate veining and compartmentalized array of stones.

NETTIE ROSENSTEIN

As a small child, Austrian born Nettie Rosenstein, (originally Nettie Rosencrans) emigrated to the United States with her family. Her career began in 1927 in millinery but, as with other of her contemporaries, it wasn't long before her talents turned to couture and later expanded into accessories.

In 1961, after several decades as one of America's premier couturiers, Rosenstein decided to discontinue her fashion line, keeping only the jewelry and accessory branches of the business, which, unfortunately, became a short-lived endeavor.

Many of Rosenstein's finest jewelry offerings are to be found in the unusual sterling and enamel designs issued during the 1930s and Forties. It's interesting to note that even during that period of slow economic recovery from a devastating economic depression, Rosenstein's jewelry was offered at prices equivalent to at least a week's pay, or more, for the average individual. Viewing them today, one can understand why, for they are the epitome of high quality and strong, imaginative designs.

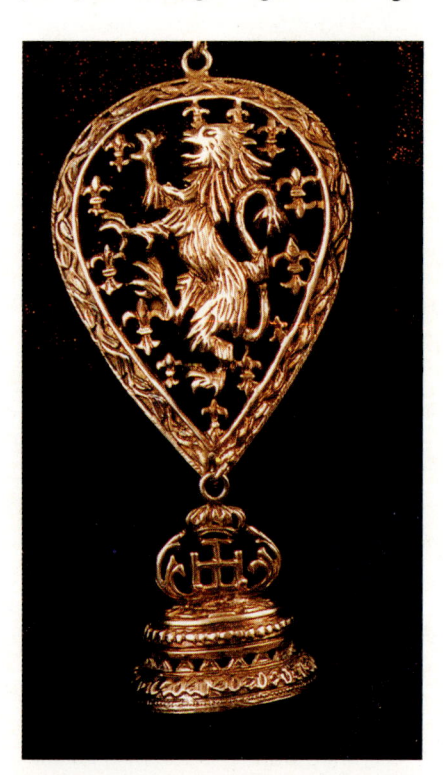

From a popular heraldic Rosenstein series of the early Forties, a crown brooch with graceful ribbon accents, a large sterling silver crest, a lion pendant with seal base, and a heavy swedged choker (note the racing chariots).

From the early 1940s, the famous Nettie Rosenstein long-stemmed pipe.

Fat cat...with faux ivory belly, golden whiskers, and rhinestone face and tail, a surrealistic feline by Rosenstein.

Rhinestones glimmer like raindrops on this duck-handled umbrella pin by Rosenstein.

Tweetie Pie...enamel and antiqued gold in a charming design by Nettie Rosenstein.

This Nettie Rosenstein sterling (vermeil) fur clip is a fine example of late Thirties/early Forties skill, coupled with an imaginative design. Enameled in a soft, very pale turquoise-green, the gold rimmed petals protect a multitude of colorful, bobbling beads.

Fanciful fruit by Rosenstein...a faux ivory apple studded with turquoise and rhinestones and its companion, a paved apple with golden leaves and matching earrings.

The always popular heart design, here in an unusual layered sterling brooch by Nettie Rosenstein; the antiqued vermeil finish is rimmed with dusky pearls converging on a blue-center stone accented with rhinestones.

A melange of jewelry from the 1950s. The shower earrings are by Brania, the five-strand necklace is from Hattie Carnegie, the antique gilt beads are by Castlecliff, and the jeweled strawberry is attributed to Nettie Rosenstein.

YVES SAINT LAURENT

Serving as an apprentice to Christian Dior provided the background for Saint Laurent's future influence in couture, initially when he was given responsibility for the first Dior line after his mentor's death, and later when he established his own fashion empire in 1962.

Venturing into the Rive Gauche boutique field in 1966 gave Saint Laurent an expanded opportunity to meet the demands of a worldwide market eager for YSL fashions and accessories (with many Dior offerings also marked YSL). Providing an exclusive "made just for you" look, usually marked with the unique interlocking YSL logo, Saint Laurent jewelry designs mirror the verve to be found in creative couture.

By Yves Saint Laurent, an enamel necklace, cleverly paired with glass bead accents, and "wild" matching earrings, both in vibrant shades of teal and fuschia. Note the faceted gold beads and carved stones on the earrings.

Yves Saint Laurent necklace of shimmery black hearts hanging from a chain with spacers in multi-shapes and styles. This parure also includes matching black heart earrings.

SANDOR

The name Sandor was derived from the first name of its founder, Sandor Goldberger. The business began in the late 1930s-early Forties, and came to an end in the mid-Seventies. Today, because of their exceptional quality and impeccable design, Sandor pieces rank among the most highly collectible examples of fine vintage jewelry from this "golden age."

This ceramic face brooch, a spoof on Josephine Baker's stage persona, dons a "chapeau" featuring poured clear resin "bananas" (a la Gripoux). Signed Sandor.

This dainty set shows yet another side to Sandor designs...tiny seed pearls, all encased in ropes of gold. A fine example of why it always pays to take a "second look."

These garnet-colored stones take on a particularly appealing glow when reflected against the coppery gradations of color in this giant Sandor bow.

A Sandor enameled geranium seems an appropriate companion to this coiffed and curled poodle.

Spring blooms in this dynamic Sandor necklace featuring a profusion of enameled flowers. Gold backed, each section is linked together with gold chain.

Delicate beauty! An intricate intertwining of gold wires supports a mass of tiny, pale yellow enameled flowers with crystal centers, all topped with three strategically-placed amethyst stones, in this 2.75" brooch and earring parure by Sandor.

SCHIAPARELLI

An icon in the field of fashion and accessories, Italian born Elsa Schiaparelli established her first couture house in Paris prior to the start of World War I, with another opening in London in 1934. She also became a mentor to such future luminaries as Cardin, de Givenchy, and Madeleine Vionnet.

Recognizing the interaction between accessorizing and fashion, Schiaparelli logically expanded her talents into costume jewelry. Here, however, she created her own remarkable aura, opening new vistas in previously uncharted waters by employing simple items like wood, string, ceramics, and feathers. The results were both wild and witty...and, as might be expected, the public was understandably intrigued! The jewelry trends that Schiaparelli pioneered are innumerable, not the least of which was the enameled flower pins that she popularized.

The list of individuals and companies responsible for jewelry designs bearing the Schiaparelli name reads like a "Who's Who" of prominent personages. They include Cecil Beaton and Giacomelli in the 1930s, and Etienne de Beaumont, who created many of the flagship shocking pink pieces that became so distinctively Schiaparelli. Jean Schlumberger, considered one of the most brilliant designers of this century in both fine and costume jewelry, was the guiding force behind many of Schiaparelli's most outstanding pieces, including the whimsical 1938 circus collection. Also involved in the creation and manufacture of Schiaparelli's jewelry were companies like Germany's Henkel and Grosse (who also did much of Dior's early jewelry), and Milan's Coppola e Toppo.

By 1954, changing economic conditions forced Schiaparelli, as they had many other prominent couture figures, to continue the successful accessory lines under licensing agreements, an arrangement that was in effect for only a few years, thus bringing to an end the prestigious offerings of Schiaparelli.

Schiaparelli at her whimsical best. Schiaparelli is credited with introducing the charm bracelet concept during the 1930s. This one has bells that ring (pearl clappers!), and the hinged purse opens, as does the "watch," making a convenient repository for a perfumed cotton ball, sachet, or even pills; the latter two are constructed of two-part castings. The fuschia and turquoise stones with pearl accents provide charming accents to a delightful piece that combines fine craftsmanship...and elan!

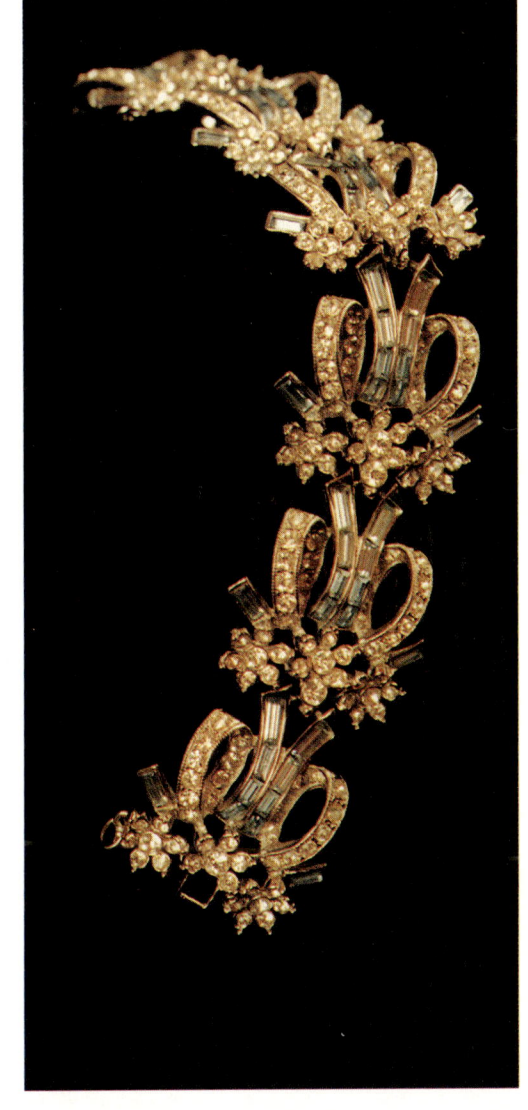

Schiaparelli sparkles.....this time in a bracelet with the look of fine jewelry.

Taking the bow-tie to another dimension...two sparkling designs by Schiaparelli.

Typical of the 1940s, a Schiaparelli brooch of pearls and rhinestones, regally perched against a glass birdbath.

Branch coral with a twist...this charmer by Schiaparelli has amethyst stones and twinkling flowers nestled in its golden branches.

Schiaparelli earrings, these in an appealing color combination of pale blue stones with lavender-hued topaz centers.

With rough-cut iridescent stones, accented by clear green stones and faux citrines, this bracelet by Schiaparelli has the unexpected mixture of materials and design for which she was noted.

Like something from an ancient treasure chest, a Schiaparelli bracelet with burnished faux mabe pearls and antiqued silver trim.

Sitting atop a rosy-pink necklace by Schiaparelli, a fuschia Schiaparelli brooch with giant winged mabe pearls.

Signed Schiaparelli, a 2.5" x 2.5" highly-domed, modeled brooch in a surrealistic orchid design, accented by dark blue montana sapphires and pavé rhinestones.

Close-up of a Schiaparelli bracelet featuring frosted, carved glass leaves in shades of topaz, smoky topaz, and cheery jonquil, intertwined by an elaborate, free-form antique gold branch.

This pair of sinuous gold and "black diamonds" blowfish are from a Jean Schlumberger design, and signed Schiaparelli.

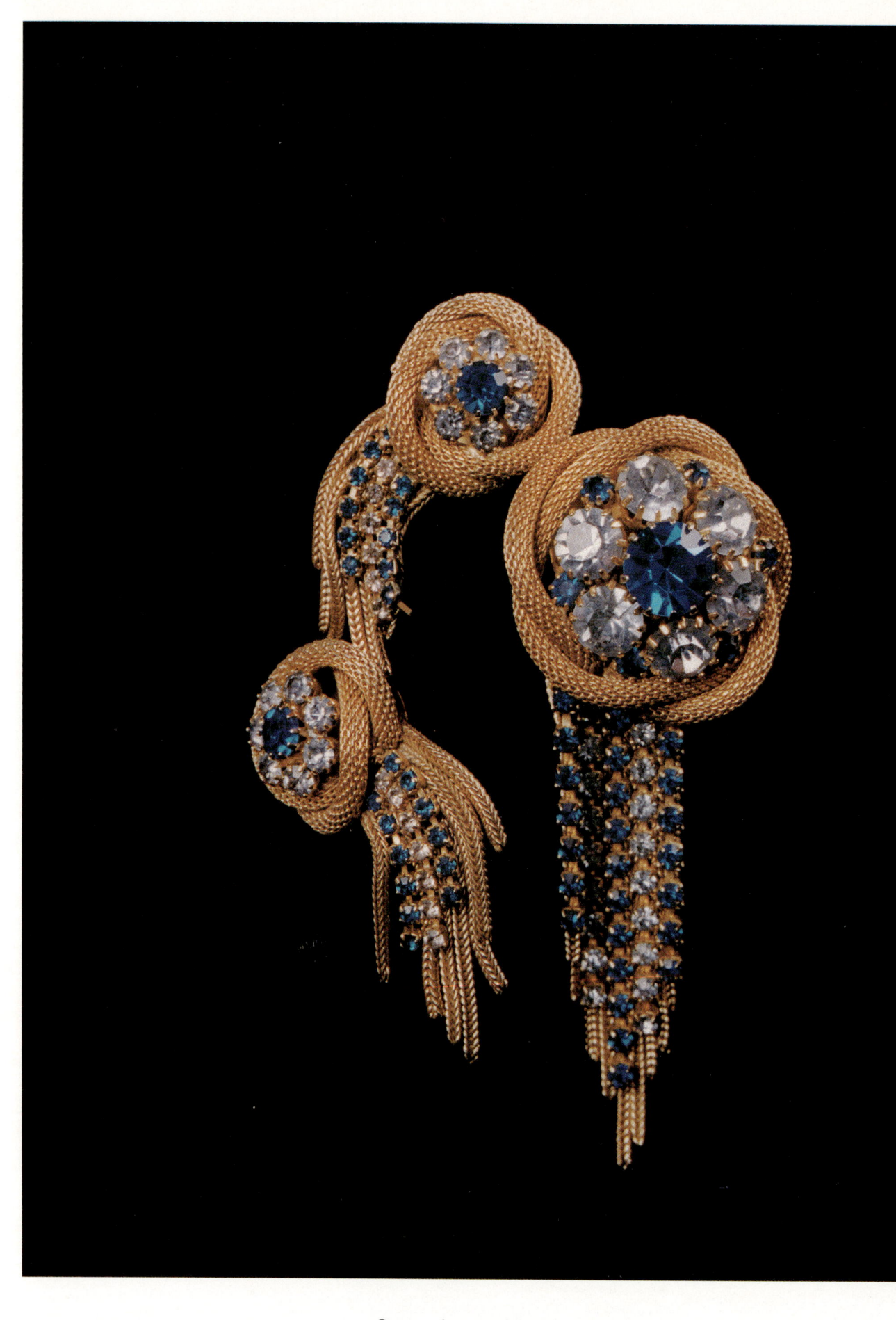

Grace and power...brooch and earrings by Schiaparelli.

Pure Schiaparelli...an ornate antiqued silver brooch, bracelet, and earrings, featuring clusters of carved red stones, stippled berries, and iridescents, all swirling madly in a design that "pulls out all the stops."

By Schiaparelli. A large, dome-shaped brooch and matching earrings...pearlized stones, soft iridescents, and enormous pale faux citrines meld into a winning combination.

Note the pearl clappers in this rhinestone bells pendant necklace by Schiaparelli.

Simple but dynamic, a Schiaparelli bracelet with huge faux sapphire stones.

SCHREINER

Henry Schreiner, as had so many of his peers, also began his "accessories" career in a related field, in this case with a shoe buckle company that flourished during the flapper era of the 1920s. The opening of his own business in 1951 was a logical progression of his past experience and skills, and he was joined in this family venture by his daughter and son-in-law, Terry and Ambros Albert. Following Henry Schreiner's death in 1954, the Alberts continued the business, with phenomenal success, until 1975. Schreiner pieces were never mass-produced and the attention they commanded in the media made extensive advertising unnecessary.

In addition to their jewelry lines, Schreiner also produced buckles, jeweled buttons, and belts. Except for a stretch belt line in the 1970s, all Schreiner jeweled belts were offered during the 1960s. Schreiner was responsible for couturier Norman Norell's jewelry and related accoutrements, and many Adele Simpson and Dior pieces are also attributable to them. With much success, Schreiner often utilized the distinctive gunmetal plating that added so much charm and beauty to the designs of this period. Their early stones were only of Czechoslovakian origin. Schreiner jewelry is highly regarded by serious collectors and is representative of some of the very finest, and most admirable, vintage jewelry to be found today.

It's magic! This 3.5" Schreiner brooch with layered white keystones and domed black and yellow center, rests atop an enlargement of the same brooch's center section. Designed in 1957 by Ambros Albert, Schreiner's son-in-law, it was called the "ruffle" brooch. Executed on two levels in cast settings, the model alone would cost at least $1000 to produce today. The keystones, which were made in Germany by Czechoslovakian craftsmen, are no longer produced, making the entire piece both cost and material-prohibitive today.

Blue on blue...this Schreiner brooch with matching earrings will turn heads today, just as it did decades ago.

This Schreiner parure has hand-set, violet-hued and turquoise stones, each encapsulated in strands of gold. A design of this type is particularly awe-inspiring since the stones had to be soldered on trays of gravel into which the preshaped mold had been poured, thus giving the piece its extreme modulation. Adding to its intricacy, the unfoiled stones necessitated a very thin shell, thereby making the entire procedure even more time consuming since a low-melt solder had to be used and special care taken not to destroy the stone. With four solder points on each of these stones, the enormity of this task becomes readily apparent.

Too hot to handle! Smoke rises from this stunning Schreiner set with its intense colorations, each bud protectively cradling a large center stone.

This Schreiner bar pin features faux watermelon tourmalines and a large, sparkling drop.

Schreiner layered brooch, with unusual, hand-set stones of varying sizes and styles, creating an understated yet dynamic image. Note the variety of the sizes and shapes of the stones (marquis, pear, rectangular, and round); the rectangular jade glass ones cannot be made today.

Three brooches, all giving credence to the versatility of Schreiner designs. The one at top left is high-domed, with unusual stone colorations (aptly called "cracked ice") accented with pearls, tiny coral beads, and a huge mabe pearl center; at top right is an openwork design in shades of pink and purple; the bottom piece features a delicate base supporting vari-sized crystals and pearls.

A "must see to believe" piece. With cleverly faceted, crystal clear stones, symmetrically offset by an intricate center section with metal-tipped spokes that match the elaborate prongs, this 3.5" brooch is a Schreiner masterpiece.

From the 1950s, a rarely seen Schreiner belt featuring pearls, blue and topaz rhinestones, and amber confetti stones, all hand-set.

SELRO

Close up of detail on a ribbed Hematite necklace and bracelet with accents and joining links of iridescent "black diamonds." An eye-catching combination by Selro.

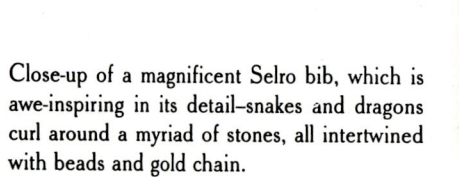

Close-up of a magnificent Selro bib, which is awe-inspiring in its detail–snakes and dragons curl around a myriad of stones, all intertwined with beads and gold chain.

ADELE SIMPSON

Jewelry that is seldom seen, an Adele Simpson necklace and earrings parure of pearls and rhinestones offset with faux aquamarines.

Made by Vogue in the late 1940s or early 1950s for Adele Simpson, and bearing her name, these snowflake pins are a rare find. Courtesy of Bernard Shapiro.

TRIFARI

Needing little introduction–even to the uninitiated–with its long and illustrious history, Trifari is probably the most recognized name in costume jewelry today. Founded in 1918 by Gustavo Trifari and Leo Krussman, Trifari's business originally concentrated on other accessory items, specifically hair ornaments and bar pins. However, during the flapper era of the Twenties and its introduction of the popular bobbed hairdo, hair ornaments lost their appeal, and practicality, causing the partners to wisely turn to the newly-emerging market of costume jewelry.

Trifari contributed his design skills and Krussman his abilities in sales and merchandising for the new venture. It proved to be a potent, and profitable, combination. In 1925, Carl Fishel became the third partner, and by 1930 their major designer was a European-trained French gentleman, Alfred Philippe, who had previously been responsible for "fine" jewelry designs for both Van Cleef and Arpels and Cartier.

The World War II years brought the public some of Trifari's finest offerings. Metal shortages necessitated their working in sterling silver, with auspicious results. These particular pieces, including the Trifari crown pin introduced in 1941, and earlier sterling pieces, are among the most highly-prized vintage jewelry collectibles today.

The company has changed hands several times since those early days, being acquired by Hallmark Cards in 1975 and then in 1988 by Crystal Brands. A year later, Monet was also absorbed by the Crystal Brands conglomerate, and in tandem with Trifari and Marvella, all now comprise the Crystal Brands Jewelry Group.

An ornate variation on the popular Trifari sterling frog, this one is encrusted with stones and has a vermeil finish.

With glimmering enamel, glittering red eyes, and polished silver trim, this Trifari "puddle-jumper" is a whopping 2.75".

Pink moonstones like giant bubbles in an ethereal Trifari bracelet.

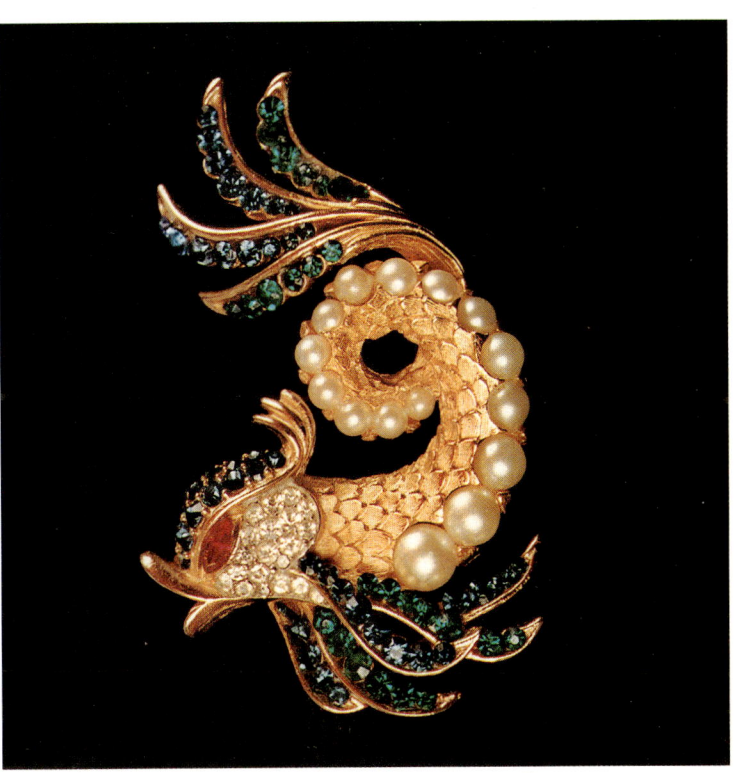

With golden scales, glittering stones, and "pearls from the deep," a mythological fish by Trifari.

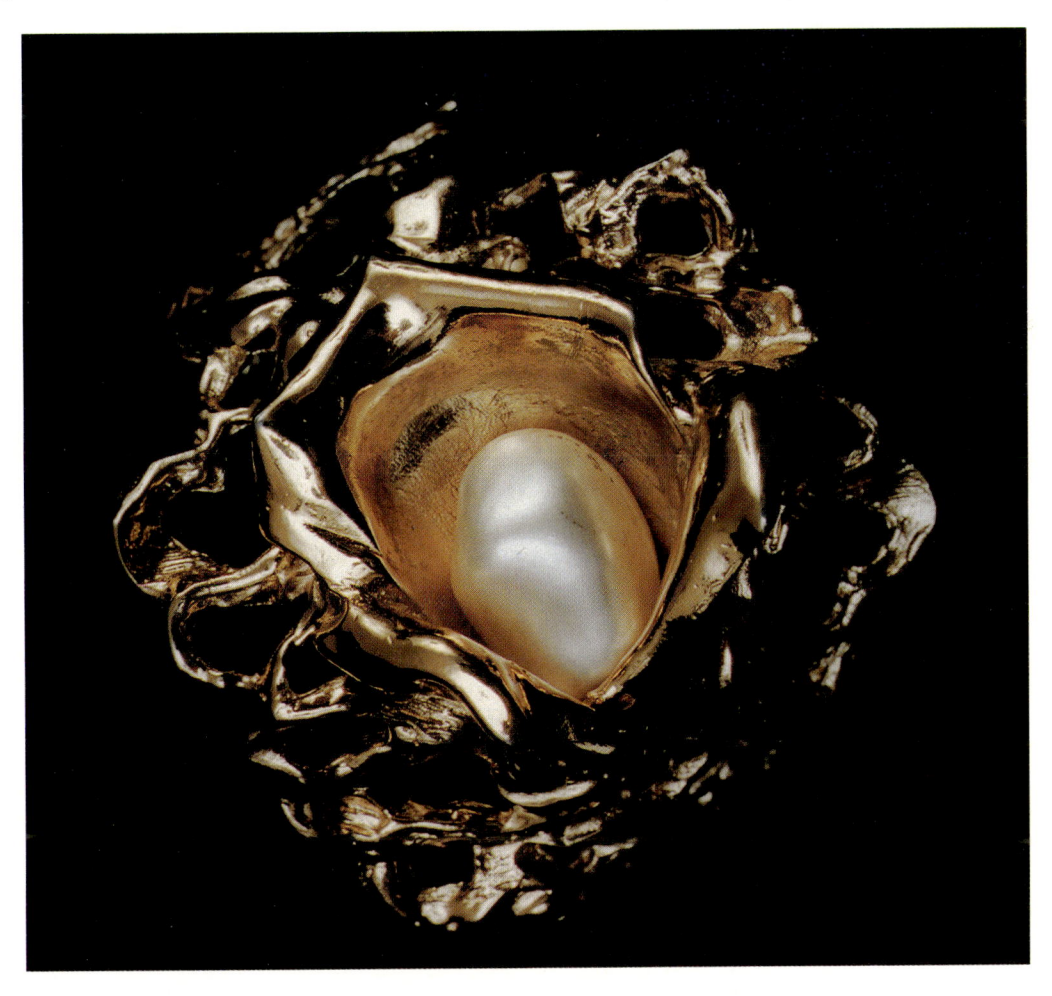

Highly-detailed, a massive Trifari cuff with giant mabe pearl nestled in its center.

Awesome! A Trifari sword brooch, approximately 3.5" in length, accentuates the classic beauty of cabochons in medieval-inspired designs.

A powerful sterling heraldic piece by Trifari.

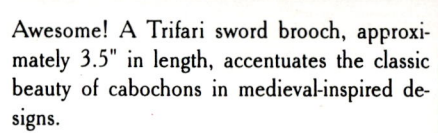

A symphony in red and white! This fur clip is a stunning example of why jewels by Trifari captivated the American woman.

An elegant Trifari brooch in sterling (vermeil) accented with emerald-cut faux rubies and pave rhinestones.

170

On the prowl! This purposeful Trifari cat is striped with undulating rhinestone bands and polished metal. And here's his counterpart...another "stalker" of similar design but without the deeper, more intricate striping.

These sleek 4" Trifari enameled panthers can be worn singly or–for the more adventuresome--together. Either way, they're "attention getters" par excellence!

171

Trifari double-plated earrings with overlapping black diamond leaves. Although designs like this might be taken for granted by the untrained eye, producing this particular pair of earrings required immense skill and knowledge of the jeweler's art.

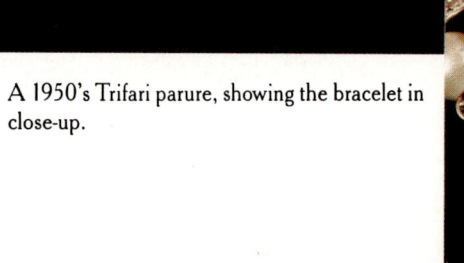

A 1950's Trifari parure, showing the bracelet in close-up.

172

Fashioned in petaled layers of pastel-hued stones,
a colorful Trifari brooch.

VOGUE BIJOUX

Of undetermined age or origin, this enormous bird is marked Vogue Bijoux. It features polished gold, long plumage, and a center stone that by itself is larger than most individual brooches.

VOLUPTE

Volupte was founded in 1926 and specifically noted for their flair in presenting ladies of the day with a wide variety of elegant compact styles, a business that continued for several decades thereafter. During this period, Volupte was also responsible for highly-stylized jewelry designs, which admirably reflected their dedication to offering only the finest of feminine accoutrements to the public. Not readily uncovered, due to the lesser quantities produced when compared to their larger counterparts in the industry, and also to their concentration on the popular compact line, finely-crafted Volupte jewelry now becomes a very special find.

This Volupté necklace has unusual crackled glass stones with a subtle hint of glitter, all mounted in gold settings.

175

WEISNER

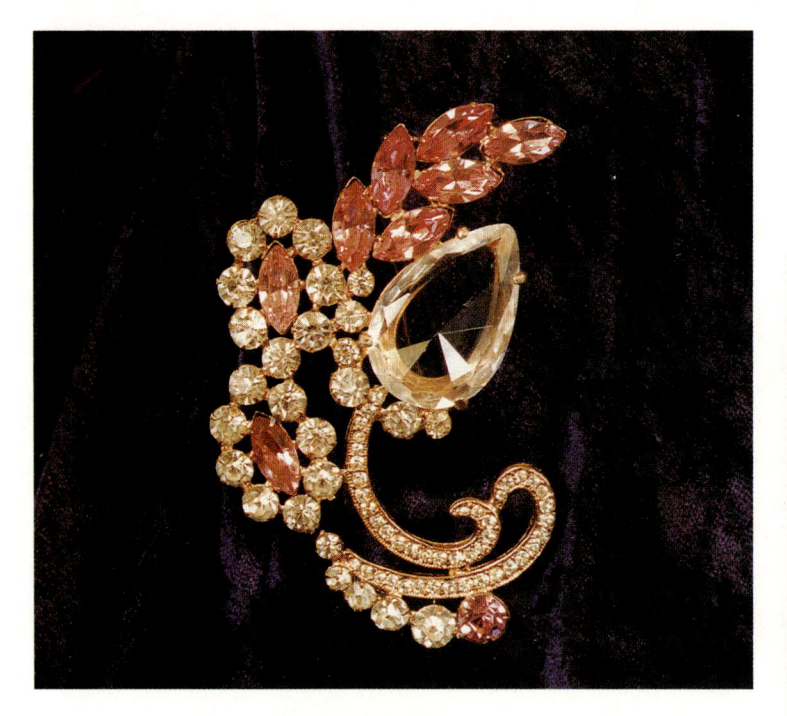

By Weisner, this 3.75" brooch features a giant stone of clear, faceted crystal, offset by rhinestones and pink ovals.

WEISS

Receiving his initiation into the costume jewelry world under the aegis of Coro, Albert Weiss founded his own company in the early 1940s. The Weiss name has since become very popular with collectors, especially due to their interesting designs, colorful stones, and generally modest price tag in relation to the quality received.

In a concave, bowl-shaped design, this Weiss brooch has stones of all sizes and shapes circling in layers until they reach the emerald-cut crystals that form a half-moon over its center.

A luscious Weiss brooch that combines three popular elements in mid-twentieth century costume jewelry...a fruit theme, enameling, and black japanned finish.

This large, square Weiss brooch has an interesting melange of stones in all sizes and shapes.

With enameled flowers and leaves, this charming Weiss brooch has a "trembling" butterfly, with japanned trim and glittering stones, hovering close by.

WHITING AND DAVIS

Synonymous with finely constructed mesh bags of gold and silver, Whiting and Davis is a Massachusetts operation harkening back to 1876. Not to be overlooked, however, were their jewelry designs, most especially the elaborate oversized cuffs and pendant necklaces. They remain in business today, still supplying evening accessories, including those in the ever-popular mesh styles.

In the genre of Art Nouveau, an elaborate cuff bracelet by Whiting and Davis.

Known since 1876 for their mesh purses, Whiting and Davis has also given us unusual jewelry designs. These cuff bracelets of burnished gold have giant stones and elaborate filigree designs reminiscent of a long ago time and place.

178

Unsigned Beauties of the Modern Era

"Indeed, collectors should be careful not to be blinded by the name game." [1]

The heyday of costume jewelry, encompassing most specifically the time between the close of World War II and its downswing during the late 1970s and early '80s, when it became an unwitting victim of the jewelry "gold rush," created a climate of frenzied activity. The demand was so great manufacturers had a difficult time keeping up with it, resulting in many pieces without maker's markings. Additionally, on many parures, the makers' name appeared on only one piece (an earring perhaps). Since paper tagging was not uncommon, the makers' name would become "lost" when the tag was removed after purchase and then tossed out, just as we do with garment tags today. Further complicating matters, many manufacturers and designers never identified their designs, even with tags. The list of these operations whose pieces now remain a mystery, either because of lost tags or no tagging at all, is enormous, and includes: Stenberg Kaslo, which was also a jobbing operation and headed by Jules Steinberg (noted for their manipulated jewelry, some of their own pieces were marked with the Bsk designation but many others remained unsigned); Imperial Pearl; Delizza and Elster (which produced high quality, large stone pieces); and Mille Fleur, to name but a few.

Consequently, there are countless examples of truly outstanding costume jewelry pieces with no identifying marks. Each is worthy of the same awe and appreciation given to the very best of their signed counterparts, and their niche in the history of this industry should in no way be diminished by their lack of identification. Serious buyers should recognize that because a piece includes a manufacturer's or designer's name doesn't automatically make it "good" or even desirable, nor should an unsigned piece automatically be relegated to "costume jewelry limbo." Many fabulous pieces have been pushed to the side or ignored because of this prejudicial attitude. It only stands to reason that much of little consequence and even questionable workmanship was bound to flood the market when demand, and the ever-present need for cost containment, reached the proportions that occurred during this time, and it was inevitable that these would include unsigned as well as signed pieces.

Although many who specialize in vintage jewelry are quick to point out the reluctance of their customers to invest in unsigned pieces, Norman Crider, a costume jewelry maven who established a worldwide clientele from his shop in New York's Trump Tower, states quite firmly that "...Without question the top ten pieces I've ever had have not been signed."[2]

The section that follows serves as a visual testimony to these sentiments.

1 *Ball, Art & Auction*, p. 115
2 Ibid., p. 115

Of sterling in coppery-hued vermeil, this brooch stands tall...and unsigned.

Heavily plated, and with the look of the Forties, this deep-hued sterling (vermeil) flower features a bold combination of colors, as seen in its large red center stone, rimmed with faux amethysts.

In the pinky-coppery glow so popular in the Forties, a giant vermeil flower.

With glistening cabochons, pearls, and rhinestones, this sunburst brooch with pendant drop would be an elegant addition to any wardrobe.

Needing no signature...a magnificent copper over sterling bow brooch with giant faux emerald center stone surrounded by tiny prong-set stones on wires.

Flying high, a glittering kite-shaped brooch combines individually encapsulated stones in an unusual three-dimensional design.

Intricate design carried to its highest level...3.5" in diameter, it needs no further explanation.

Towering 4", this sterling trumpet flower brooch has symmetry of design that ranks it among the very best...signed or unsigned.

A symphony in black and crystal. This enormous 5.25" unsigned Deco-style bow is elegance (and verve) personified!

Unsigned, this glamorous necklace holds a secret, for here is a fine example of the versatility of detachable pieces, this one offering three different possibilities: it can be worn as shown; the large center section can be detached and worn separately as a glittering evening brooch; and the necklace can also be worn without the attachment, for a more subdued look.

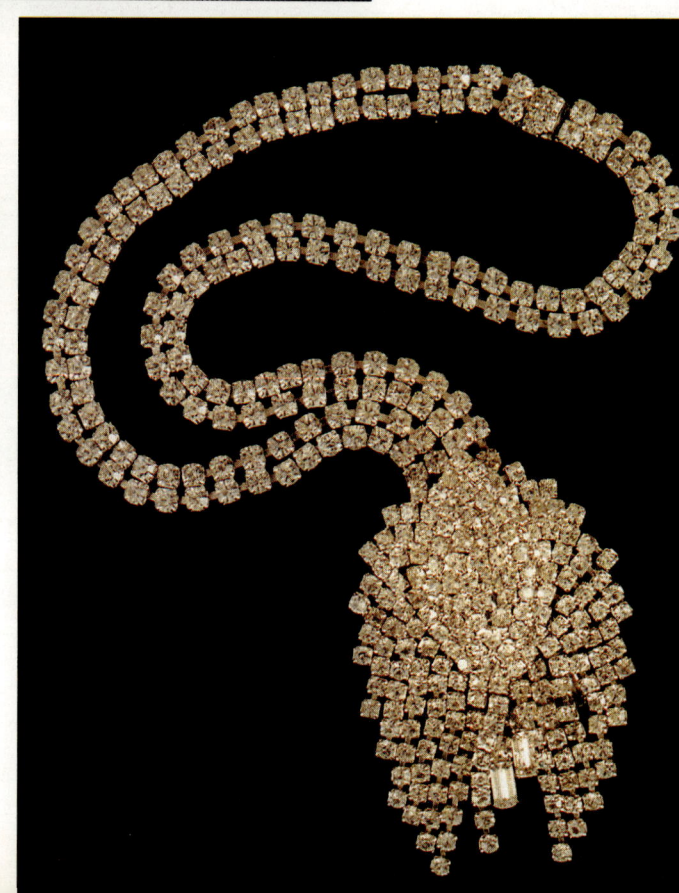

This stunning color combination is well-suited to the gold-rimmed, soft blue glass petals with their vivid fuschia centers. A parure from the 1930s-early Forties period, it consists of a bracelet fashioned on a graceful flexible gold frame, a 3.5 x 3" fur clip, and matching earrings. Astoundingly beautiful, it has the look of Chanel's floral glass designs.

Not for the feint of heart, this 1.75" bracelet boasts a dynamic mix of faux topaz keystones and crystals.

"The eagle has landed"...this giant fellow is a commanding presence, whether atop a mountain peak or sitting proudly on a garment lapel.

This glittering 5" pinwheel of flowers reminds one of a cascading waterfall or a fourth of July pinwheel

This composition Deco ring box, decorated in the style of the Thirties, holds a showy cocktail ring with unusual curved center stone.

Unsigned, this large, high-domed fur clip is in the same design genre as the Robert piece previously shown. It gives clear evidence that "unsigned" jewelry can be just as beautiful and labor-intensive as their signed counterparts. This design was also used quite effectively in many outstanding Hobé pieces.

This French enamel parure is most unusual...the giant lapis blue stone, framed in gold, is encircled with row after row of tiny glass beads. What appear to be Italian mosaic blue and white beads are also caged in an intricate arrangement of individual compartments, from which hang gold and lapis beads. The matching earrings and ring complete a stunning ensemble.

186

With the look of Hobé, but unsigned, a locket brooch with silver antique finish accented by "milky" moonstones.

A Danish vermeil cuff bracelet with very strong, free-form design.

In the pinky-coppery glow so popular in the Forties, a giant vermeil flower.

Unsigned (but possibly attributable to Ferragamo), a close up of a bracelet of flowing, golden leaves.

A handful...this heavily-plated bow brooch is from the 1930s.

Imagine this on your wrist...here are rows of glittering rhinestones and baguettes, in a combination that needs no signature to make any audience "stand up and take notice."

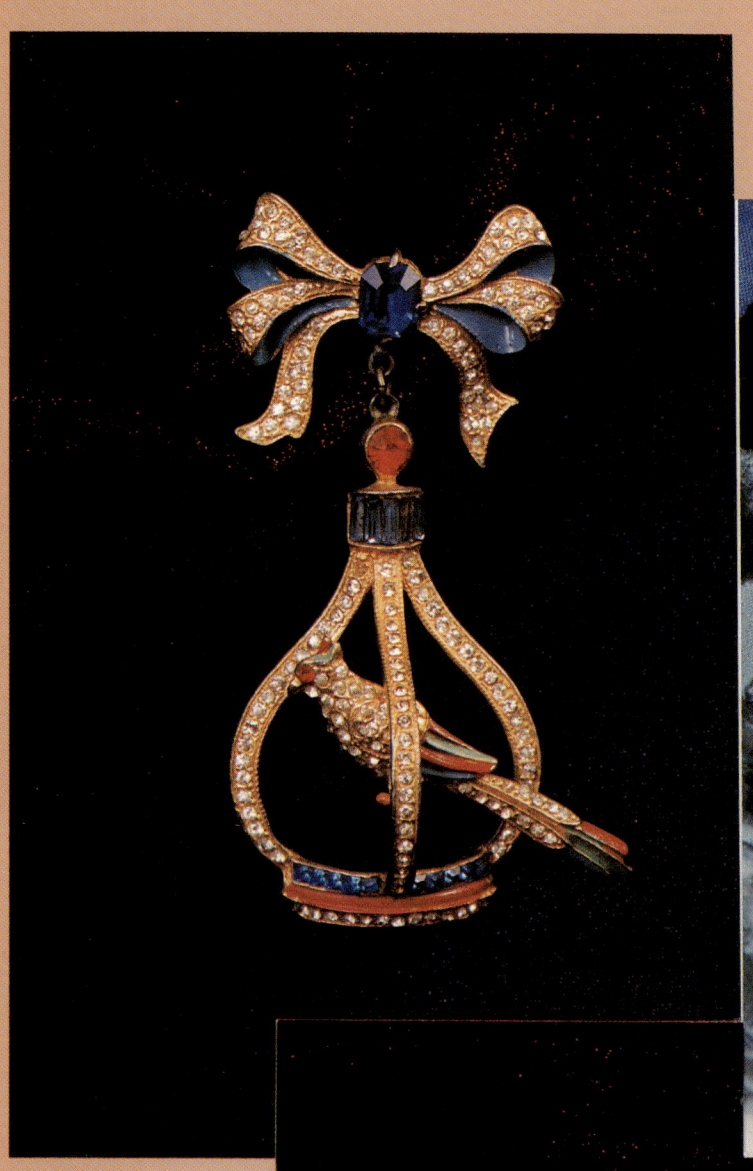

"It was only a bird in a gilded cage"...a whimsical charmer with no name but lots of character!

Swirls and flowers in layer after layer of stones in an appealing combination of complementary colors. Marked simply "Austria."

Enameling and glitter, all used effectively in this lead-backed brooch from the 1930s.

A magnificent piece that takes the term "unsigned" to new heights, and what better vehicle to accomplish the task than this 4" feathered and bejeweled bird that's large enough to fit in the palm of one's hand!

Fire and Ice! In a daring color combination, this bracelet has huge red stones rimmed with double rows of red and pink.

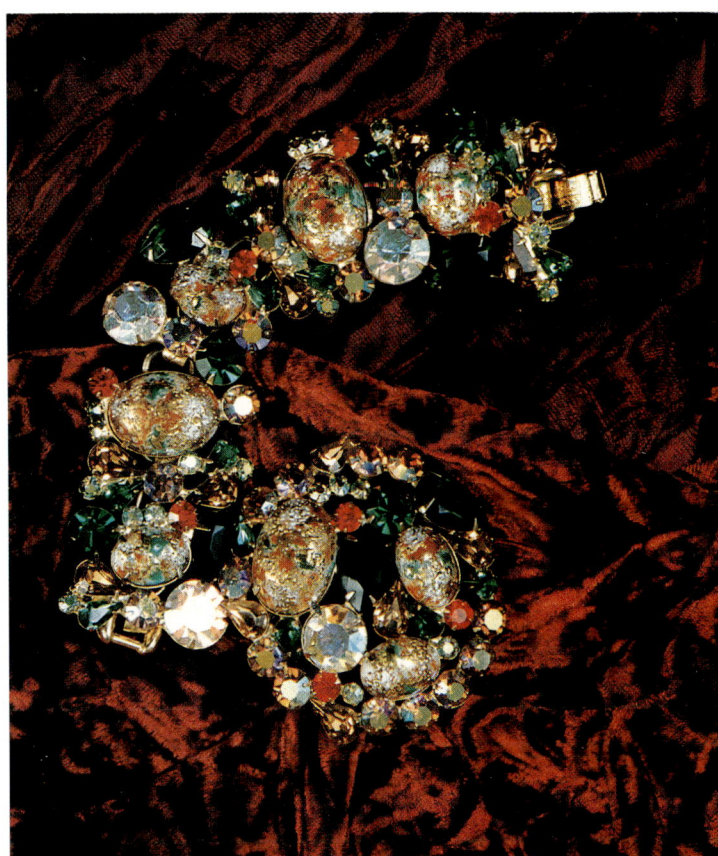

Unsigned, a bib, earrings, bracelet, and brooch of multi-style stones and brilliant combinations of colors. The close-up gives added impetus to the detail and versatility in this truly remarkable example of the jeweler's art.

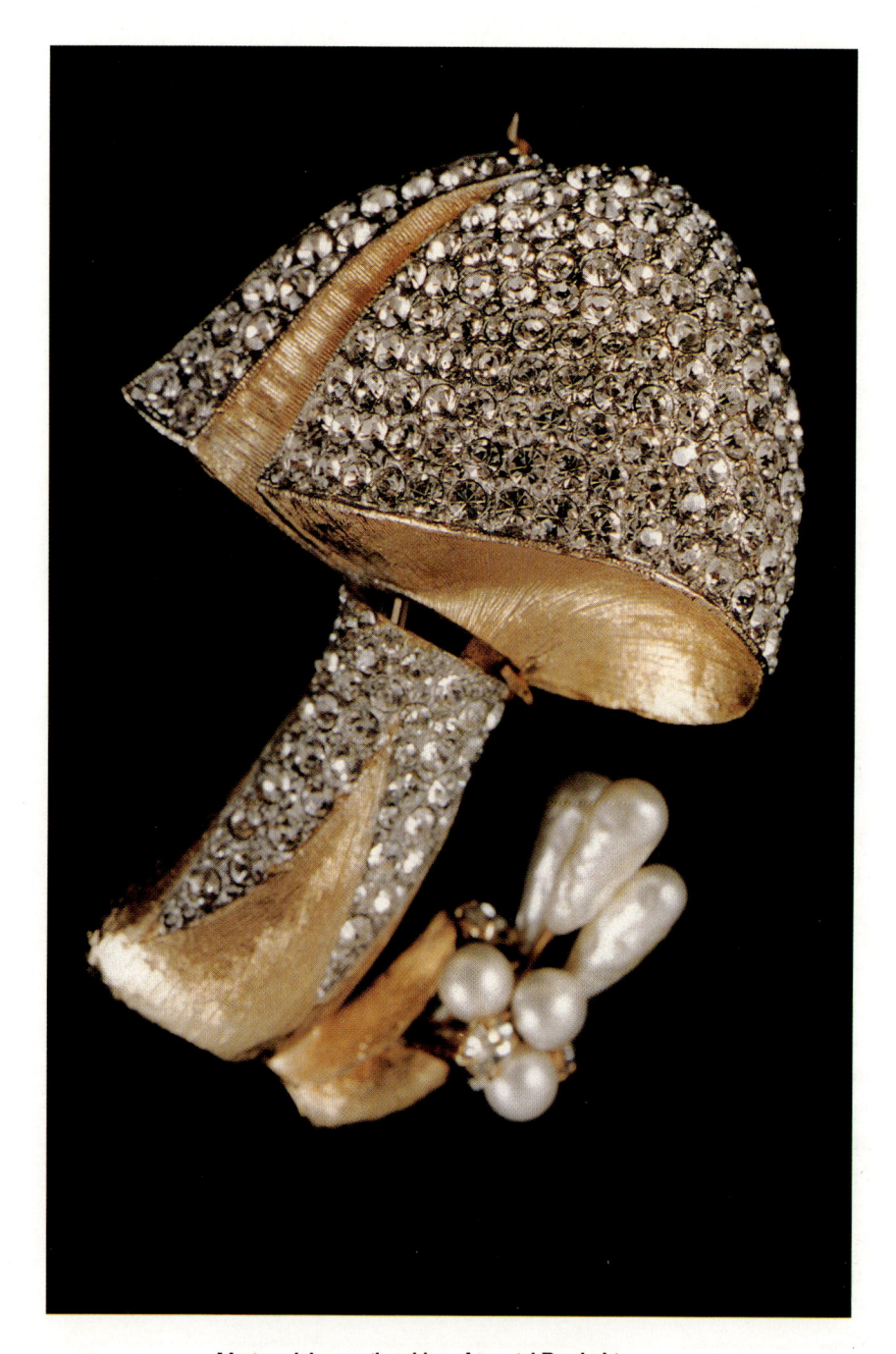

Unsigned, but attributable to Imperial Pearl, this pavé mushroom with wing pearls at the base is an outstanding example of the power of an imaginative, graceful design.

Newer...and Notable

The artistic spirit is an ever-changing, ever evolving one, with each generation offering innovative designs and carrying former concepts to previously unexplored heights of creativity. How fortunate that many of the foremost designers of what we now refer to as vintage costume jewelry are still working their magic today! How fortunate, too, that new designers and artists continue to weave their own spells, constantly bringing glorious examples of new looks in upscale jewelry that transcend restrictive labels.

Jewelry manufacturing operations proliferate today, and those serving the so-called "mass market" are entrenched in a highly competitive business. Countless talented and imaginative designers are now creating in this volatile environment, and we show here a sampling of the works of artisans currently or recently designing for small shops ("boutique settings") or their own premises. All give credence to the fact that, as in other artistic endeavors, there will always be a parade of budding "master creators" who, with infinite patience, are compelled to go that extra mile to think and rethink and to build and rebuild. In the process those "buds" blossom forth, some in subtle, understated shapes and hues, others in bold bursts of color and intensity.

Here, once again, a new chapter in the history of jewelry is being written, not only with the designs, but often in a glorious–and sometimes daring–intermingling of both manmade and natural materials. Thus, the evolution of the jewelers' art is an ever-changing one, leaving little doubt that wondrous concepts will continue to enchant present and future audiences, all eager to feast their eyes on yet another jewelry masterpiece!

From Karl Lagerfeld's Marco Polo line, this brooch makes a most successful "exploration" into the art of design, with its brilliant enameling, pearl and luminescent stone accents, and intricate detailing. Note the gold rosettes and bows on the shoes and stockings and the gold "embroidery" on the coat.

Sippin' nectar! With an unusual combination of colors, so artfully handled by Thelma Deutsch, this graceful bird covers the palm of one's hand.

With japanned backing that adds impetus to the strong colors, this 3" bow brooch is by Thelma Deutsch.

No bed of roses...or is it? This whimsical Thelma Deutsch giraffe, in a particularly imaginative 3.5" design, seems sublimely happy.

Vivienne Westwood's "favorite piece of jewelry"...a 1995 design. Photo by Nick Towers.

Like a patriotic UFO, a Thelma Deutsch triangular brooch, tastefully accented with red and blue stones.

From France. Faces in the crowd...Alexis LeHellec contemporary earrings and matching stickpin, both of cast plastic with pearls.

Fabulous! With semi-precious stones, glass cabochons and glass cameos, this sterling (vermeil) rope and earrings by Lazaro is indicative of the fine quality and workmanship available to today's discerning buyer.

By Mark Spirito. With the look of Ancient Rome, three styles of earrings fashioned with semi-precious stones and a vermeil finish.

Like Byzantine discs, hammered gold, faux citrine, and confetti-stone earrings by Karl Lagerfeld.

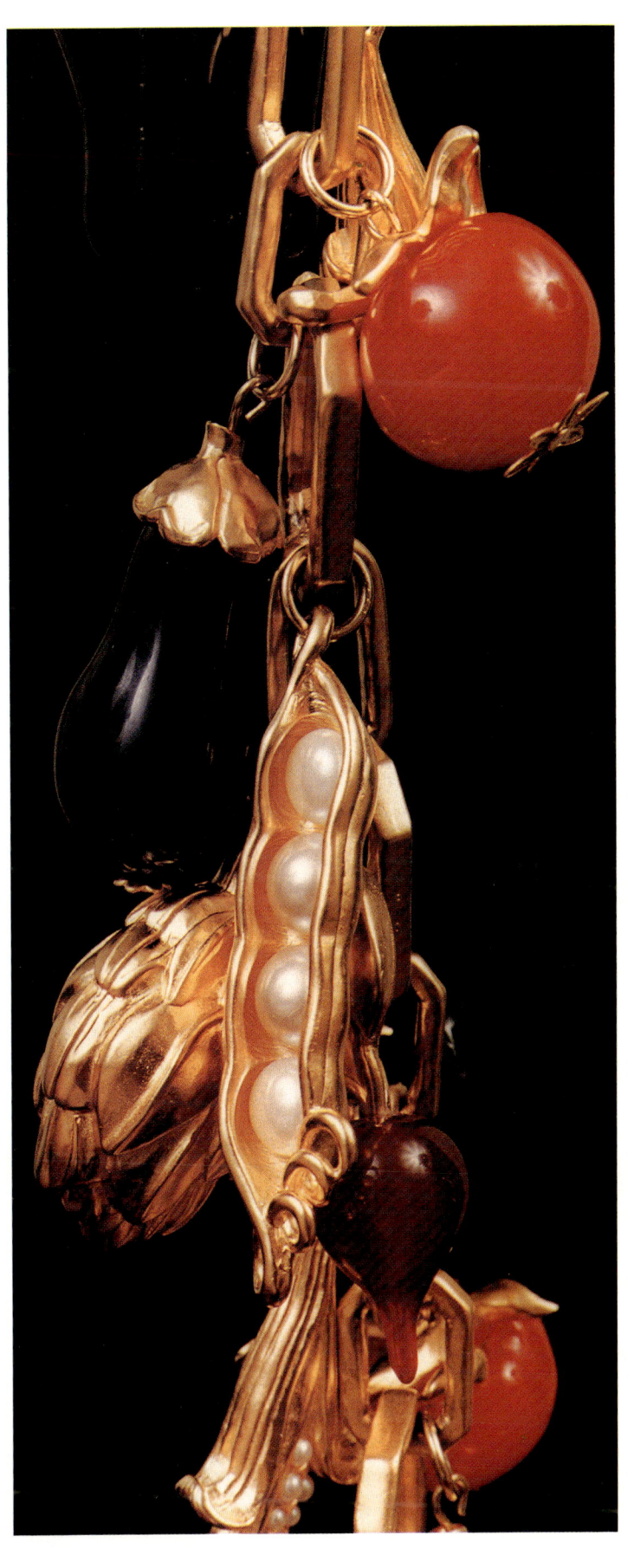

A vegetarian delight! This close-up of a Karl Lagerfeld bracelet is a symphony of design...with cherry tomatoes, eggplants, radishes, and "pearl-filled" peapods.

From the 1980s, Isabel Canovas brings her unique imagination to a glossy wooden turtle with cross-hatched red back and elaborate gold accents. The red and black ladybug earrings, also by Canovas, provide a striking contrast.

With a Spanish influence...and good enough to eat, Isabel Canovas created this scrumptious necklace and its unusual matching hair ornament.

By Adjani Moini. A stupendous 6.5" in length, this hand-fashioned brooch, with close-up of the nacreous chrysanthemum petals, is reflective of the imagination and finite workmanship Moini brings to all his exclusively designed and executed pieces.

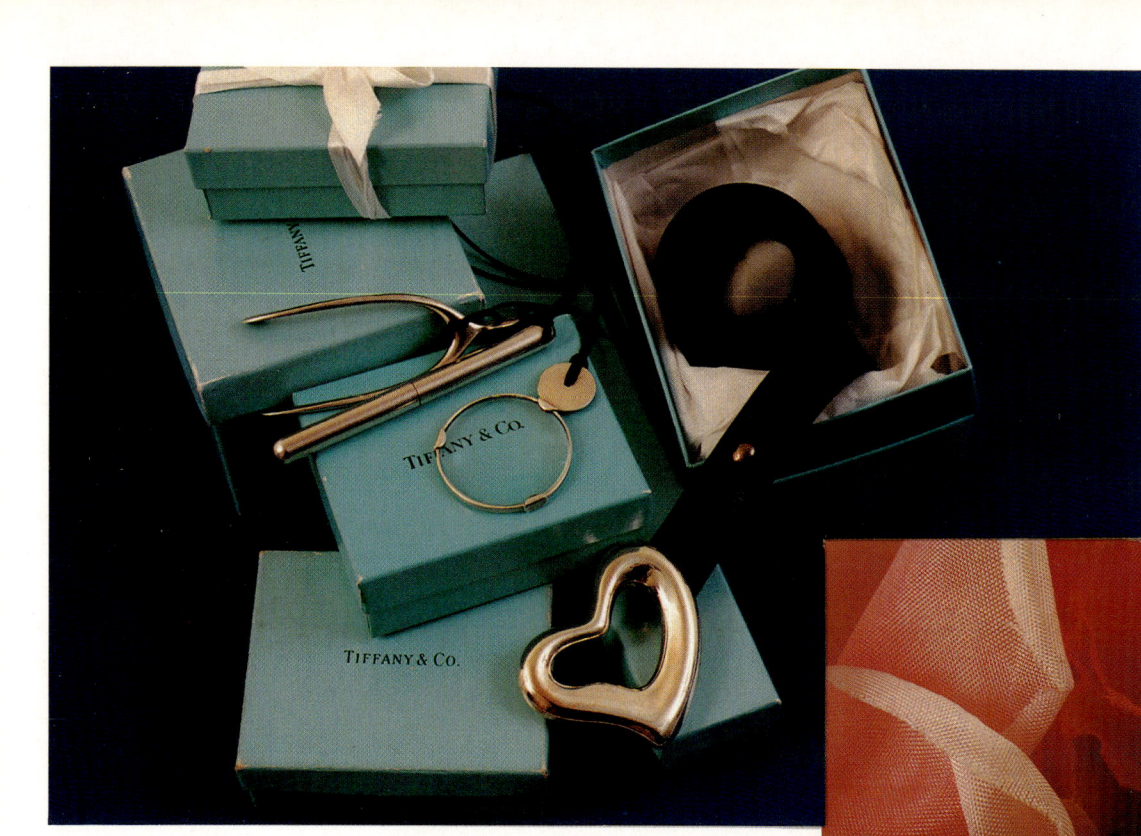

Elsa Peretti classics, all in sterling...wishbone pendant, magnifying glass, pen, and belt.

Shown here is a 3" locust brooch by Butler and Wilson, a British company highly regarded in the international marketplace for their upscale designs and discrimintating clientele. The current interest in costume jewelry featuring elaborate stone work makes this piece particularly noteworthy.

Like chandelier ornaments from another era, these ropes by Erickson Beamon are of sparkling crystals in a multitude of shapes and sizes, all strung on thin, black leather strips.

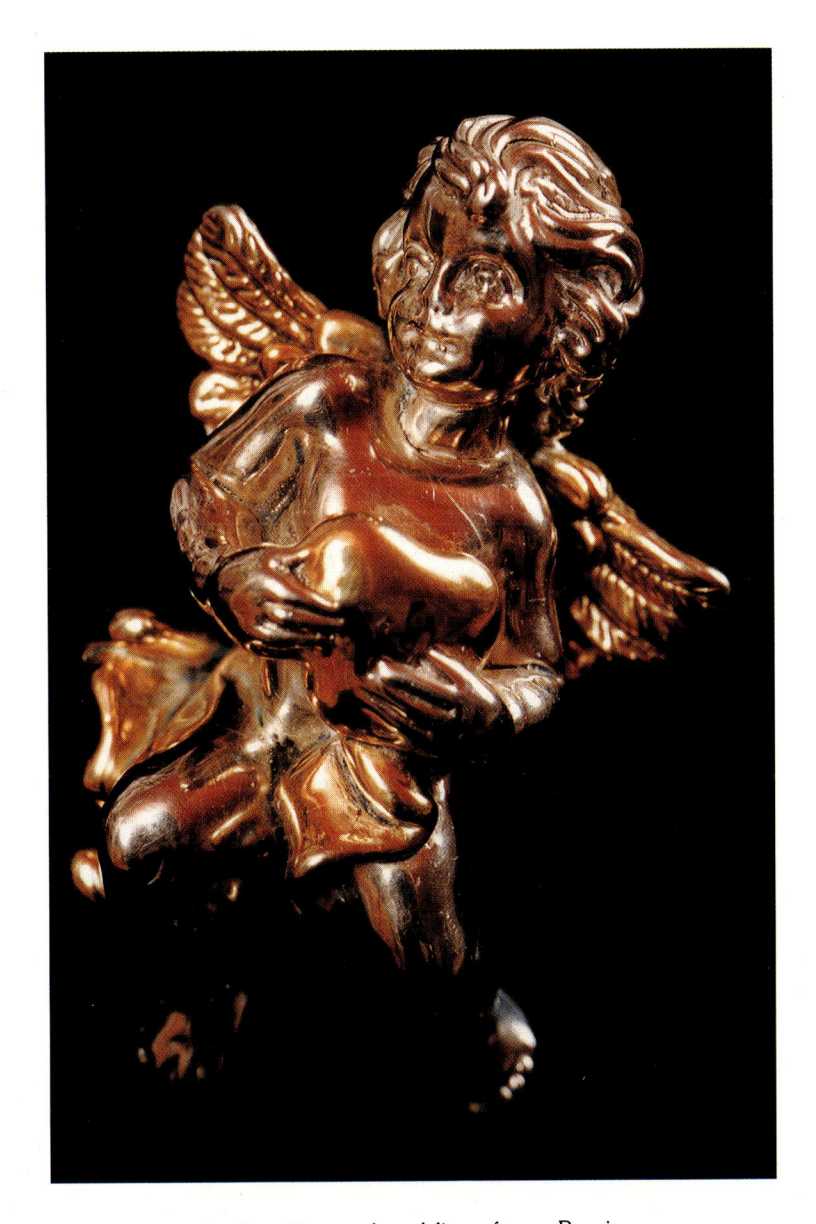

Looking like an ethereal figure from a Renaissance painting, but of modern vintage, this Italian brooch is a companion to the one pictured on the Frontispiece.

Bibliography

Adams, Cynthia. *Traditional Home*; 'Diamonds a la Deco'; Des Moines, Iowa; Meredith Corporation, Holiday 1994.
Ball, Joanne Dubbs. *Art & Auction*; 'Costume Jewelry Soars'; New York; December 1990.
Ball, Joanne Dubbs and Torem, Dorothy Hehl. *The Art of Fashion Accessories*; Atglen, Pa.; Schiffer Publishing, 1993.
Becker, Vivienne. *Fabulous Costume Jewelry*; Atglen, Pa.; Schiffer Publishing, 1993.
Cera, Deanna Farneti. *Jewels of Fantasy*; New York; New York; Abrams, 1992.
Cirino, Antonio and Rose, Augustus. *Jewelry Making and Design*; New York; Dover Publications, Inc., 1967.
Faberge Arts Foundation. *Faberge: Imperial Jeweller*; Washington, D.C., 1993.
Fisher, Alexander. *The Art of Enamelling Upon Metal*; London; Bradbury, Agnew & Co., 1906.
Hughes, Graham. *The Art of Jewelry*; New York; Studio Vista Publishers, 1972; Gallery Books, W.H. Smith Publishers, Inc., 1984.
Inside Antiques. Glendale, California, October 1994.
Lanllier, Jan and Pini, Marie-Anne. *Five Centuries of Jewelry*; New York. Leon Amiel Publisher, 1983.
Liban, Felicia and Mitchell, Louise. *Cloissone Enameling and Jewelry Making*; New York. Dover Publications Inc., 1989.
Miller, Harrice Simons. *Official Identification and Price Guide to Costume Jewelry*; New York. House of Collectibles, 1990.
Miller, Harrice Simons. *The Confident Collector: Costume Jewelry*, 2nd Edition; New York. Avon Books, 1994.
Moro, Ginger. *European Designer Jewelry*; Atglen, Pa. Schiffer Publishing, 1995.
Mulvagh, Jane. *Costume Jewelry in Vogue*; London. Thames and Hudson, 1988.
Remenih, Maurine. *Enameling*; New York. Galahad Books and Nash Publishing.
Robins, Bill. *An A-Z of Gems and Jewelry*; New York. Arco Publishing, 1982.
Steele, Valerie. *Women of Fashion*; New York. Rizzoli, 1991.
Sterling Publishing. *Gemstones*; New York. 1988
Van de Lemme, Arie. *A Guide to Art Deco Style*; London; Quintet Publishing Ltd., 1986.
Vintage Fashion & Costume Jewelry Newsletter; Glen Oaks, N.Y.
Von Neumann, Robert. *Design and Creation of Jewelry, The*; Radnor, Pa. Chilton Book Co., 1982.

Price Guide

Prices vary immensely according to the condition of the piece, the location of the market, and the overall quality of the design and manufacture. Condition is always of paramount importance in assigning a value. Prices in the Midwest differ from those in the West or East, and those at specialty antique shows will vary from those at general shows. And, of course, being at the right place at the right time can make all the difference.

All these factors make it impossible to create an absolutely accurate price list, but we can offer a guide. The prices reflect what one could realistically expect to pay at retail or auction.

The left hand number is the page number. The letters following it indicate the position of the photograph on the page: T=top, L=left, R=right, TL=top left, TR=top right, C=center, CL=center left, CR=center right, B=bottom, BL=bottom left, and BR=bottom right. The right hand column of numbers are the estimated price ranges in United States dollars.

Page	Position	$ Value
18	L	150-175
18	R	100-150
19	L	150-200
19	C	200-250
19	R	100-150
20	L	125-175
20	C	125-175
20	R	175-225
21	L	100-150
21	R	100-150
22	TL	350-500
22	TR	200-275
22	B	400-600
23	TL	300-400
23	TR	250-350
23	B	150-200 each
24	TL	300-400
24	TR	450-650
24	B	175-250 each
28	T	200-250
28	B	150-200 each
29	B	175-250
31	TL	125-250 each
31	TR	175-225
32		125-175
34		225-300 pair
35		275-350
36		200-300 each
48		200-250
49		175-225
50	TL	300-350
50	TC	125-150
50	TR	175-250
50	B	75-125
51	TL	300 up-brooch / 500 up-necklace
51	TR	300 up
51	CR	350 up
51	B	300 up
52	TL	350 up
52	TR	350 up
52	BL	300 up
52	BC	400 up
52	BR	300 up
53		1000 up
54	R	300-400
54	L	275-350
55	T	250-325
55	BL	200-275
55	BR	275-375
56	TL	500 up
56	LC	300-400
56	RC	250-300
56	BL	175-250
56	BR	175-225
57	TL	200-275
57	R	275-375
57	BL	1000 up
58	T	250-300
58	BL	225-325
58	BR	150-200
59	T	350-450 set
59	BL	175-225
59	BRT	200-250
59	BRB	250-350
60	T	700 up
60	B	350-500
61	TL	150-200
61	TR	100-150
61	C	175-225
61	BR	225-325
62	T	150-200 each
62	B	500 up
63	T	250-300 set
63	B	2500 up
64	TR	2000 up
65		2500 up (necklace) / 1500 up (cross) / 1000 up (brooch)
66	TL	2000 up
	TR	1000 up
	BL	1000 up
	BR	1000 up
67	TL	1800 up
67	TR	1000 up
67	BL	1200 up
67	BR	1500 up
68	TL	1200 up each
68	TR	1800 up
68	B	1000 up
69	T	700 up
	B	1200 up
70	TL	100-150 each
70	TR	350-500
70	BL	200-300
71		500 up
72	TL	200 up
72	TR	250 up
72	BL	200-300 each
72	BR	300 up
73	TL	150 up
73	TR	300 up each
73	BL	200-300
73	BR	300 up
74	TL	300 up
74	TR	350 up
74	B	800 up
75	TL	400 up
75	TR	350 up
75	BL	400 up
75	BR	200-300
76	T	175-225
76	C	125-175
76	B	150-200
77	TL	200-275
77	TR	250-325 set
77	BL	125-175
77	BR	250-350
78		350-500
79	L	300-400/set
79	R	200-275
80	T	1000 up
80	CL	175-225
80	CR	150-200
80	B	200-250
81		1200 up
82	TL	250-350
82	TR	250-300
82	B	500 up
83	B	400 up
84	TL	700 up
84	TR	600 up
84	BL	1000 up
84	BR	800 up w/box
85	TL	700 up
85	TR	600 up
85	BL	600 up
85	BR	700 up
86	TL	800 up
86	TR	700 up
86	B	1000 up/set
87		700 up/set
88	TL	350-500
88	BL	200-300
91	TL	150-200
91	TR	100-150
91	BL	250-350
91	BR	125-175
92	TR	175-250
92	BL	150-200 each
92	BR	225-300
93	T	400 up
93	C	500-600
93	B	350 up
94	TR	250-350
95		400 up
96	TL	500 up
96	TR	900 up
96	B	350 up
97	TL	500 up
97	TC	350-450
97	TR	250-300
97	BL	300-400
97	BC	225-300
97	BR	375-500
98	TL	450-600
98	TR	450-600

Page	Pos	Value
98	B	1200 up/set
199	TL	800 up
99	TR	200-275
99	CL	200-275
99	CR	700 up
991	B	600 up
101	T	2000 up/each
101	B	3000 up
102	TL	1000 up
102	TR	800 up/set
102	B	3000 up
103	T	800 up
103	B	2000 up
104	TL	800 up
104	TR	800 up
104	C	800 up
104	BL	1200 up
105	TL	500 up
105	R	700 up
105	BL	1500 up
106	TL	800 up/set
106	TR	500 up
106	BL	800 up/each
106	BR	500 up
108	TL	200-275
108	TR	225-300
108	BL	150-200
108	BR	200–300

Note: Only Joseff retail pieces will be valued.

Page	Pos	Value
112	TR	1500 up
112	BR	800 up
113	T	2500 up
113	B	800 up
117	TL	75-125 each
117	C	300 up
117	BL	800 up
117	BR	l: 1000 up; r: 800 up
118	TL	300-400
118	TR	200-300
118	B	200-300
119	TL	350-450
119	TR	500 up
119	B	125-175
120	TL	500-700 set
120	TR	150-200 set
120	BL	250-300
121	TL	400 up
121	TR	200-300
121	BL	800 up
121	BR	400 up
122	T	250-350
122	CL	600 up
122	CR	400 up
122	BR	175-225
123	TL	800 up
123	TR	200-275
123	BR	300-375
124	TL	350-450
124	C	350-450
124	B	350-450
125	T	300-400
125	C	200-300
125	BL	300-500
126		175-250 each
127	TL	400-500
127	TR	125-175 each
127	BR	300-375
128	TL	175-225
128	TR	700 up
128	B	800 up
129	TL	175-225
129	TR	100-150
129	B	100-125 pair
130	TL	750 up
130	CT	250-350
130	CB	600 up
130	BL	450 up
131	T	100-150
131	BR	250-350
132	T	275-375
132	BL	200-300
133	T	150-200
133	BL	175-250 each
134	TL	225-300 each
134	TR	175-225 set
134	CL	175-225 set
134	CR	300-400 set
135	TC	400-500
135	TL	275-350 set
135	BL	150-175 set
135	BR	300-375
136	TL	500-700
136	TR	275-350 set
136	BR	225-300
137	TL	300-400
137	TR	300-400
137	BL	275-375
137	BR	175-250
138	TL	325-400
138	CR	450-600
138	BL	150-200 set
139	T	400-500
139	BR	175-250
140		75-175 each
141	TL	150-175 each
141	TR	200-300 pair
141	B	125-175
142	TL	300-400
142	TR	200-250
142	BL	250-300
142	BR	350 up
143	TL	800 up
143	TR	600 up
143	BL	600 up
144	TL	300-400
144	TR	350-500
144	BL	350-450
144	BR	400-600
145	TL	700 up
145	TR	300-400
145	CR	250-350
145	BL	350-500
146	TL	350-500
146	CL	350-500 set
146	TR	600 up
146	BL	350-450
148		t: 200-300; b: 550-700
149	TL	275-325 set
149	TR	175-225 set
149	B	400 up
150	TL	350-450
150	TR	225-275
150	BL	1000 up
150	BR	200-300
151	T	700 up
151	B	350-500
152	T	500 up
152	B	175-225
153	TL	250-350
153	BL	300-400
153	R	350-450
154	TL	250-350 brooch
154		300-500 necklace
154	TR	300-400
154	B	600 up
155	T	300-375
155	B	500 up/pair
156		350-425 set
157		700 up/set
158	TL	1000 up/set
158	TR	500 up
159		350 up
160		700 up
161		300-375 set
162		300-350 set
163		350-450 set
164	TL	200-275
164	C	175-225
164	BL/T	l: 275-350; r: 175-225;
	BL/B	$250-300
165	T	600 up
165	B	900 up
166	L	450-600 set
166	R	800 up
167	T	450-600
167	BR	300-375 pair
168	T	500 up
168	B	300-400
169	TL	350-500
169	TR	350-450
169	B	300-400
170	TL	500 up
170	TR	300-400
170	C	350-500
170	BR	400 up
171	TR	300-375
171	CL	275-350
171	B	700 up/pair
172	TL	800 up/set
172	TR	175-225
173		350-425
174		1000 up
175		200-275
176	TL	150-175
176	TR	250-325
176	B	125-150
177	TL	275-375
177	CR	150-200
178	T	75-125
178	B	l:125-175; r: 175-225
180	TL	300-375
180	TR	175-225
180	B	175-225
181	T	250-300
181	CL	300-400
181	CR	200-250
181	B	375-500
182	T	700 up
182	C	375-500
182	B	450-600
183		1000 up
184	TL	400-600
184	BL	225-275
184	R	250-300
185		300-400
186	L	300-400
186	R	500 up/set
187		275-350
188	TL	175-250
188	TR	300-400
188	B	150-200
189	T	250-300
189	B	450-600
190	TL	200-300
190	TR	400-500
190	B	175-250
191		1000 up
192		175-250
193		1500 up
194		150-175

Note: Jewelry of current vintage will not be valued.

Page	Pos	Value
196	TL	300-400
196	TR	500 up
196	B	300-375
197	B	200-275
200	TL	l: 250-350; r: 75-125
200	B	t: 1500 up; b: 750 up

Index

Accessocraft, 49, 50
Agnini, Oreste, 132, 133, 134
Agnini and Singer, 132, 133
Agnini, Oreste, 82
Albert, Terry, 160
Albert, Ambros, 160
American Style Co., 50
Anthony Creations, 71
Apisdorf, Irving, 58
Aquilino, Anthony, 71
"Around the Word in Eighty Days," 111
ART, 50

Baker, Josephine, 149
Barclay, McClelland, 51, 52
Barclay, 51
Beamon, Erickson, 202
Beaton, Cecil, 151
Belle-Sharmeer, 62
Berlin iron jewelry, 33, 43
Bijoux Cascio, 53
Bloomingdale's, 53
Bonaparte, Napoleon
Bonwit Teller, 53
Boucher, 54, 55
Boucher, Sandra, 54
Boucher, Marcel, 54
Brania, 56, 81, 147
Braque, Georges, 58
Brody, Steve, 56
BSK, 179
Burks of Canada, 56
Butler and Wilson, 202

Cadoro, 56, 57
Calvaire, 57
"Camille," 110
Canning Jewel, 124
Canovas, Isabel, 200
Capri, 80
Capucci, 53
Caque, Monsieur, 33
Cardin, Pierre, 151
Carey, MacDonald, 116
Carnegie, Hattie, 57, 58, 59, 147
Cartier, 78, 168
Cascio, Ricardo, 53
Cascio, Gaetano, 53
Castlecliff, 60, 61, 62, 147
Canovas, Isabel, 200
Caviness, Alice, 63
Chanel, 31, 63, 64, 65, 66, 67, 68, 69, 77, 183
Charles Lindberg Museum, 132
Chernow, Jay, 131

Chernow, Michael, 131
Chorbajian, Joseph, 107
Ciner, 70
Ciner, Emanuel, 70
Circle Products, 49
Clark, Robert, 78
Clio Novelties, 40, 127
Cohn and Rosenberger, 71
Coppola e Toppo, 151
Coro Duette, 74, 75
Coro, 71, 72, 73, 75, 176
CoroCraft, 71, 72, 73, 74, 76
Crawford, Joan, 113
Crider, Norman, 179
Crystal Brands, 131, 168
Czar Nicolas II, 81

Darnell, Linda, 109
Davis, Bette, 110
Deauville Beads, 40
de Beaumont, Count Etienne, 63, 151
de Givenchy, Hubert, 92, 151
DeLillo, 78
DeLillo, William, 78
Delizza and Elster, 179
De Mario, 79, 81
De Mario, Robert, 79, 139
De Rosa, 79, 80
De Rosa, Elvira, 79
De Rosa, Ralph, 79
De Rosa, Theresa, 79
De Rosa, Virginia 79
Detkin, William, 40
Detkin, Paul, 40
Deutsch, Thelma, 196, 197
Devarrone, Simion Pierre, 33
Di Nicola, 80
Di Nicola, Jerry, 80
Dinglinger, John Melchior, 13
Dior, Christian, 148, 151, 160
Dior by Kramer, 119, 120
Duke of Verdura, 63, 81

Edward III, 12
Effront, Nadine, 58
Eisenberg, 82, 83, 84, 85, 86, 87, 88, 89, 90, 133
Eisenberg, Karl, 83, 88
Eisenberg, Jonas, 82
"Elizabeth and Essex," 110
Ellen Designs, 139
Empress Eugenie, 102, 103
Eugene, 91

Faberge, Carl, 13, 26, 27, 35
Fishel, Carl, 168
Fashion Institute of Technology, 54
Fashioncraft, 139
Fath, Jacques, 92
Ferragamo, Salvatore, 188
Fialkoff, Frank, 94
Finkelstein, Sol, 139
Fisher, Alexander, 33
Florenza, 91
"Forever Amber," 109
Francoise, 71, 77
Furst, Clifford, 60

Gablonz of Bohemia, 39, 40
Garbo, Greta, 110
Garson, Greer, 115
GemCraft, 71
Giacomelli, 151
Gibson girl, 21
Givenchy, 92
Glass, Leo, 93
Goldberger, Sandor, 149
"Gone With the Wind," 110
Goosens, Robert, 63
Grand Duke Dmitri, 63
Great Gambini, The, 114
Gripoix, 31, 63, 64, 65, 67

Hallmark Cards, 168
HAR, 93
Harry Winston, 78
Haskell, Miriam, 78, 79, 94, 95, 96, 97, 98, 99, 139
Hazard, Archie, 107
Hazard, Jack, 107
Henkel and Grosse, 151
Henri Bendel, 53
Hervey, Irene, 111
Hess, Frank, 78
Hess, Frank, 94
Hobe, 100, 101, 102, 103, 104, 105, 106, 187
Hobe, Donald, 100
Hobe, Jacque, 100
Hobe, James, 100
Hobe, Robert, 100
Hobe, William, 100
Hollycraft, 107, 108
Hughes, Graham, 26, 46

Imperial Pearl, 40, 179, 194
Iribe, Paul, 31
Isadora, 108

Jaffe, David, 139
Jaffe, Ellen, 139
Janvier, 41
Jomaz, 130
Joseff, Joan Castle, 41, 110
Joseff, Eugene, 41, 110
Joseff of Hollywood, 41, 109, 110, 111, 112, 113, 114, 115, 116, 117, 118
Josephs, Larry, 58
Joy, Lester, 126

Kamke, Ruth, 83
Kaplan, Robert, 40
Kasoff, Dan, 91
Kasoff, Larry, 91
Katz, Adolph, 71, 76
Kinsler, Morris, 94
KJL for Laguna, 123, 124
Korda, Alexander, 118, 119
Kramer, 119, 120
Kramer, Harry, 119
Kramer, Louis, 119
Kramer, Morris, 119
Krussman, Leo, 168

Lagerfeld, Karl, 195, 199
Laguna, 40
Lalique, 18, 26
Lancaster, Burt, 116
Lane, Kenneth Jay (KJL), 120, 121, 122, 123, 124
Lawrence, Jody, 116
Lazaro, 198
"Le Gazette du Bon Ton," 32
Ledo, 125, 128, 129
Leiber, Judith, 125
LeHellec, Alexis, 198
LeLong, Lucien, 92
LePape, 32
Les Bernard, 125, 126, 127, 128
Levy, Robert, 79, 139
Lindberg, Anne Morrow, 132
Lindberg, Charles A., 132
Lindner, E., 63
Lisner, 71, 129
Lord & Taylor, 53
Lucien Picard, 136

MacLaine, Shirley, 111
Marie Antoinette, 110
Marion, Helen, 76
Markle, William, 60
Marvella, 168
Mazer, 130
Mazer, Joseph, 130
McCardell, Claire, 58
Mimi d 'N, 56, 79, 81, 82
ModeArt, 50

Moini, Adjani, 201
Monet, 131, 168
Moonan, Peggy, 58
Moss, Sanford, 94
"Mr. Peabody and the Mermaid," 111

Napier, 131, 132
"New Yorker, The," 10
Niven, David, 111
Norell, Norman, 57, 160

O'Neil, Barbara, 115
ORA, 82, 132, 133, 134

Panetta, 135
Panetta, Amadeo, 135
Panetta, Armand, 135
Panetta, Benedetto, 135
Paris Exposition, 26
"Patient in Room 18, The," 112
Pausback, Raymond, 133
Pennino, 135
Pepper, Arthur, 50
Peretti, Elsa, 202
Philippe, Alfred, 168
Poiret, Paul, 31
Powell, William, 111
Prince Albert, 40
Pucci, Emilio, 53

Queen Victoria, 40
Queen Elizabeth, 115

Rader, Pauline, 136, 137, 138
"Random Harvest," 115
Regency, 138
Reinad, 138
Reja, 139
Renaissance, The, 16
Ricci, Nina, 78
Rive Gauche Boutique, 148
Robert Originals, 58, 139, 140, 141, 142, 143, 186
Rodelheimer, Edgar, 50
Romanoff, Prince Alexander, 81
Rosenstein, Nettie, 144, 145, 146, 147
Royal Bead, 40

Saint Laurent, Yves, 148, 149
Sandor, 149, 150
Scaasi, Arnold, 81
Schiaparelli, 31, 63, 78, 81, 92, 151, 152, 153, 154, 155, 156, 157, 158, 159
Schinkel, Karl Friedrich, 33
Schlumberger, Jean, 151, 155
Schreiner, 160, 161, 162, 163, 164, 165
Schreiner, Henry, 160
Selro, 166

Shapiro, Bernard, 125, 126, 128
Shapiro, Harold, 125, 129
Shearer, Norma, 110
Sheridan, Ann, 112
Simpson, Adele, 160, 167
Singer, Ralph, 132
"South Seas Sinner," 116
Spirito, Mark, 199
Steinberg Kaslo, 179
Steinberg, Jules, 179
Steinman, Paul, 50
Steinman, Theodore, 50
Steneskieu, Dan, 56
Stevens, Lois, 63
Swarovski, Daniel, 40, 81, 83

Tecla Pearl, 30
"Ten Tall Men," 116
"Thief of Bagdad, The," 118, 119
Tiffany, 21
Tobin, Genevieve, 114
Torem, Milton, 49
"Tower of London," 115
Trifari, 131, 135, 168, 169, 170, 171, 172, 173
Trifari, Gustavo, 168
Trigere, Pauline, 58
Tutankhamen, 88
Twain, Mark, 12
Twain, Olivia, 12

Van S. Authentics, 58
Van Cleef and Arpels, 168
Vendome, 71, 76, 77
Verneuil, Auguste, 40
Verrecchia, Gene, 71
Verrecchia, Reno, 71
Victoria and Albert Museum, 224
Vionnet, Madeleine, 151
Vivien Leigh, 110
Vogue, 125, 126, 127, 128, 129, 167
Vogue Bijoux, 174
"Vogue", 10, 63
Volupte, 175

Warner Bros., 112
Weisner, 176
Weiss, 176, 177
Weiss, Albert, 176
Werkstatte, Weirner, 27
Westwood, Vivienne, 197
Whiting and Davis, 178
Whitney and Rice, 131
Wilson, Marie, 117
Winters, Shelley, 116

Young, Selwyn, 71